Spitfire at War

Spitfire at War

Alfred Price
F. R. HisT. S.

London
IAN ALLAN LTD

First published 1974

ISBN 0 7110 0560 5

Published by Ian Allan Ltd, Shepperton, Surrey,
and printed in the United Kingdom by Ian Allan
Printing Ltd.

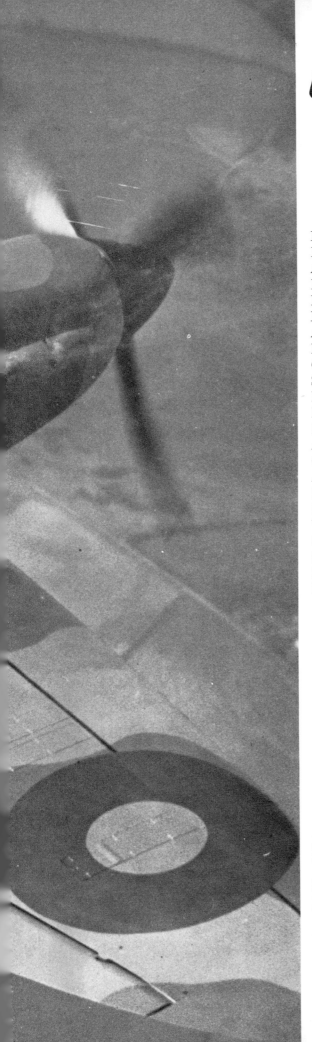

Contents

Foreword 7
Introduction 8
A Fighter is Born 10
Into Service 14
First Encounter 22
Battle of Britain 30
A Day to Remember 36
Feeding the Guns 40
Circus 62 48
Spitfire Spyplane 56
Production Testing 64
Eagle Squadron, Eighth Air Force 74
Mediterranean Spits 82
An Aerodynamicist's View 92
Gunfire Spotter 106
Achtung! Jabo! 110
Foe Without Mercy 116
Spitfire Dive-Bomber 124
When Spit Fought Spit 138
Spitfires and Guerillas 144
Stronger, Safer, Swifter 148
Spitfire Swansong 158
Photo Credits 160

A fine close-up of Supermarine's Senior Test Pilot Jeffrey Quill at the controls of the six-hundreth production Spitfire, serial P 9450, during her test flight in April 1940. This aircraft went to No 64 Squadron and later took part in the Battle of Britain.

This book is dedicated to the men and
women who transposed the Spitfire — a
mere fabrication of aluminium alloy,
steel, rubber, perspex and a few other
things — into the centre-piece of an epic
without parallel in the history of
aviation.

Foreword
Wing Commander
R. R. Stanford-Tuck, DSO DFC

When Alfred Price invited me to write a foreword to this book I was, of course, honoured; but I had the passing thought "Oh dear! Another air book to wade through".

My fears were quite unfounded. As soon as I had read the first few pages I was held by it and read on almost non-stop till I finished with Maffre's excellent 'Spitfire Swansong'.

I think the average member of the public during the war thought of Spitfire pilots as being gay, carefree, beer-swilling types, rather like the rugger club members one could see being very noisy in any pub on a Saturday night. Indeed, with a very few exceptions, nothing could have been further from the truth. Wartime flying and especially air combat in Spitfires was a very cold, calculating, 'cat and mouse' affair. Woe betide any fighter pilot who was casual or who day dreamed — he would very soon 'cop it up the back end', or one of his pals would. However, in spite of their deadly business, the Spitfire pilots had one great advantage — their aircraft — which they came to love in that strange way that men will love their cars or boats.

I got my hands on a Spitfire for the first time on a crisp morning in December 1938. It belonged to No 19 Squadron at Duxford. From the first moment I sat quietly in the cockpit, going through all the instruments, cockpit checks, take-off and landing procedures, etc, I thought "If it comes to a war, this is the girl for me." Later that day, after my first flight, I felt this even more and for the first time in any aircraft I felt I was really part of it.

Just over a year later the tremendous thrill of getting my first Me 109 over Dunkirk justified my high opinion of the handling and fighting qualities of the Spitfire. As the years went past she carried me through countless combats and difficult situations and gave of her utmost every time it was demanded. She was a true thoroughbred.

I was so enthralled reading this book and recalling the memories it brought back of the airmen I had known, the flying, and the wonderful spirit which existed in those years, that I was very tempted to write considerably more; but that is not my part in this book.

All I can say, with sincerity, is that this is a fine book about a fine aircraft and fine men and add my thanks to Alfred Price for asking me to write these few words.

January 1974
Sandwich, Kent.

Introduction

Few would dispute the contention that the Spitfire was the most famous aircraft ever to serve in the Royal Air Force. Yet why should the Spitfire have been placed on a pinnacle, so that she overshadows other aircraft whose achievements were scarcely less significant? The reasons are many, as I shall try to show on the pages which follow.

Without doubt, the Spitfire was good. Reginald Mitchell's original design was sound to the point of brilliance, with an outstanding and fundamental simplicity. After Mitchell's tragic and untimely death Joseph Smith took over the leadership of the Supermarine design team and set about exploiting the Spitfire's potential. It reflects the greatest credit on the engineering staff that the often far-reaching improvements were incorporated without disrupting the flow of production.

The resultant fighter remained in production for twelve years which bracketted the hardest-fought and technically most innovatory war in history. No other airframe design was ever so continuously, aggressively, thoroughly and successfully developed. And no less successful and thorough was the parallel development of the two Rolls Royce engines, the Merlin and the Griffon, which powered the Spitfire.

At the end of its development life the Spitfire carried an engine giving more than twice the power and weighing about three-quarters more than the original, had had its maximum take-off weight more than doubled, its fire-power increased by a factor of five, its maximum speed increased by a quarter and its rate of climb almost doubled. Except for one notable hiatus, when initially it came up against the Focke Wulf 190, the Spitfire remained unsurpassed as a short-range air-superiority fighter for almost the whole of the nine years following its first flight; moreover, it remained in front-line service in the Royal Air Force for nine years after that.

When production finally ended, in 1949, a total of more than twenty-two thousand Spitfires and Seafires had been built. It served in more than thirty air forces on six continents; more than a thousand were delivered to the Soviet Air Force and a similar number went to the US Army Force.

When appraising the historical significance of a combat aircraft, the Spitfire cannot be considered in isolation; it must be compared as fully as possible with equivalent enemy aircraft. For this reason I have included verbatim accounts from the reports on wartime comparative trials between various marks of the Spitfire and captured examples of the Messerschmitt 109 and the Focke Wulf 190 and between the Seafire and the Japanese Zeke. Generally, though not invariably, the Spitfires and Seafires could hold their own with their contemporaries. To show that technology marches on, however, I have also included an account of the battle trial between a Spitfire and a Mach 2 Lightning; as is to be expected, the former was outclassed.

So far I have spoken only of the measurable ingredients of the Spitfire's greatness. More subjective, but equally important, are the memories of those who flew her. Those I have spoken to relate that she was a sheer delight to fly, and without exception speak of their association with the Spitfire with pride and infectious enthusiasm. No form of active warfare is clean; but surely one of the least dirty is that of the fighter pilot, who sallies out into the sky to defend his homeland and loved ones.

The war itself provided further leavening for the Spitfire's lustrous reputation. How many other fighters has the Royal Air Force possessed which, for a time at least, had a performance superior to those in any other air force? But because there was no war they came and went almost un-noticed by the man in the street. Had there been no Second World War, it is almost certain that the Spitfire would have remained just one more of those pretty little fighters whose aerobatics delighted the crowds at air displays. The Spitfire achieved prominence not only because of what she could do, but because it was available at a time when Britain's needs — both defensive and morale — were greatest.

Yet there were other aircraft about which many of these things could have been said, but which never possessed the glamour of the Spitfire. In truth, the Spitfire achieved fame in such gigantic measure because she touched the very heart of the nation. She became the symbol of defiance during the grim days of the war and those who flew her were acclaimed as the valorous champions of their time. One rather unfortunate result was that the Spitfire came to overshadow much around her particularly, during the Battle of Britain, its comrade-in-arms the Hurricane. Despite the fact that the Hurricane was present in far greater numbers, saw much more of the action and shot down somewhat more enemy aircraft during the battle, a surprisingly large number of people still believe that the Spitfire almost alone won the great fight for survival in 1940.

When thinking of the Spitfire one's mind automatically turns to the well-known aces who flew her, men like 'Johnnie' Johnson, Douglas Bader, Robert Stanford-Tuck and Al Deere. These men have already told their stories in books which have, rightly, come to be numbered amongst the classic works on aerial warfare; but I am sure that they would agree that, even collectively, their own experiences represent only a minute fraction of those on the Spitfire which are worthy of recollection. To prevent repetition, therefore, in this book I have made use of accounts of those who, though less-well-known, also played important parts in the Spitfire story and who, in some cases, can judge her from viewpoints rather different from those of the fighter ace. I should like to take this opportunity to express my deep gratitude to those whose accounts appear in this book: Air Commodore Cozens, Colonel von Reisen, Group Captain Oxspring, Warrant Officer Tandy, Mr Alex Henshaw, Mr Ervin Miller, Mr Frank Hercliffe, Captain Law, Wing Commander Costain, Mr Raymond Baxter, Sir Morien Morgan, Wing Commander Middlebrook, Mr Eric Newton and Air Vice Marshal Nicholls. The words are theirs, I merely wrote them down. I am also grateful to Mr Ronnie Mogg for permission to use a verse from 'Fighters at Dawn'.

In choosing photographs for this book my primary aims have been to pick a selection which will give the broadest view of the Spitfire and the sort of war in which she fought and also to do full justice to her beauty. In respect of the last I believe that Charles Brown's pictures are without equal. I make no apology for using some of his photographs which have been published before; they are the work of a true artist and I cannot believe that their appearance here will give other than pleasure. For the other photographs, I have been extremely fortunate in having many good friends who generously lent me unpublished material from their collections. In particular I should like to tender my thanks to Jim Oughton, Derek Wood, Chris Shores, John Taylor, Mike Garbett, Brian Goulding, Charles Cain, Chaz Bowyer, Roger Freeman, 'Jackson' Dymond, Alex Lumsden, Bob Jones and Bruce Rigglesford. Most of all I should like to thank Ted Hooton, for his welcome encouragement and sound advice, for his painstaking checking of my manuscript and captions and for the rescue operation he mounted one cold, dark night. Credit is also due to Mike Brooke, who produced the line drawings.

Finally, I should like to thank my dear wife Jane for creating the domestic conditions which make authorship possible.

ALFRED PRICE

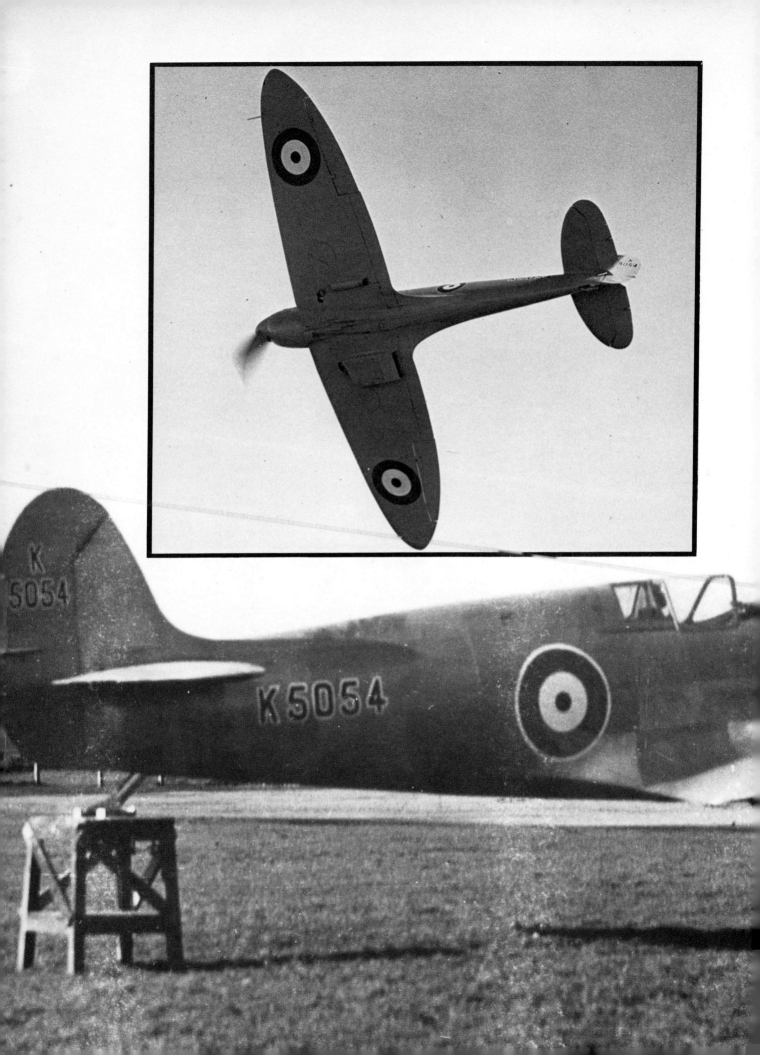

A Fighter is Born

Below: Reginald Mitchell, the Chief Designer at the Supermarine Company, led the team which created the Spitfire. Dogged by ill-health throughout his time on the project, he died in June 1937 at the age of 42 having seen only one example of the fighter completed, but with the knowledge that more than 300 were on order for the RAF.

Right, Below right: On March 22nd 1937 the prototype was undergoing high 'G' turns and looping trials from Martlesham Heath, to test the effectiveness of modified elevator gearing to overcome previous elevator buffeting. Suddenly the oil pressure fell to zero on the gauge and the engine began to run rough; the pilot cut the engine, and skilfully belly-landed the precious new aircraft on heath land beside the Woodbridge-Bawdsey road. The aircraft suffered only superficial damage and was easily repaired. Examination of the engine revealed that several connecting rods and big-ends had failed and the former had punched large holes through the crankcase. The cause of the trouble was oil starvation due to the application of 'G' and as a result the oil system of subsequent Merlins was modified. Note the changes in detail made to the prototype, since her first flight: the reduced size of the rudder horn balance, the new exhaust manifolds, the fitting of a castoring tail wheel instead of the skid, and the installation of the armament of eight machine guns (the muzzle flash eliminators of two of the Brownings can be seen protruding through the leading edge of the starboard wing). Note also the two raised panels above the trailing edge of the wing, to indicate to the pilot that the flaps were down; later Spitfires would have only a single panel on each wing for this purpose.

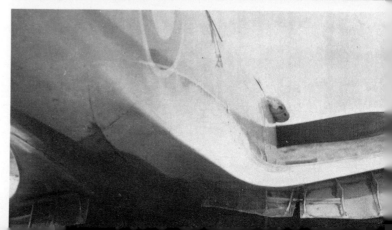

Left, Below left: The prototype Spitfire seen in her original form, pictured at the airfield at Eastleigh near Southampton probably just before her first flight on March 5th 1936. At this time the aircraft was unpainted and lacked fairings for the undercarriage legs; the gunports were empty, except for the port outer which housed the pitot tube.

Below: One of the most beautiful ever taken of the Spitfire, this photograph by Charles Brown depicts the prototype in the autumn of 1937 after she had been fully modified to Mark I standard; note the distinctive triple exhaust manifolds, a feature of the early marks of this aircraft. Like all the Charles Brown photographs in this book, this one was taken with a Zeis Palmos plate camera with a maximum shooting rate of about one per minute. Amongst his friends this cumbersome piece of equipment was something of a joke, but few people laughed at the results he achieved with it.

Into Service

Air Commodore
Henry Iliffe Cozens, CB AFC

Henry Cozens leading six of
his brand new Spitfires in
formation, for the benefit of
an official photographer in a
Blenheim, on October 31st
1938. The squadron number
on the tails was painted on
shortly before this flight and
was removed soon afterwards.

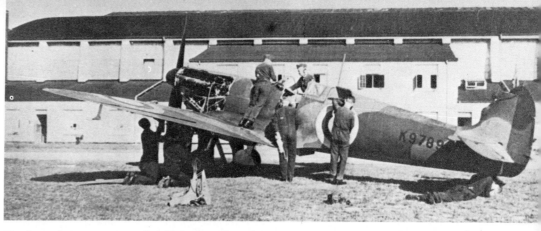

Right: K9789, the first Spitfire
to be delivered to No 19
Squadron, arrived on August
4th 1938. She was to remain
in front-line service until
1941, when she was sent to
No 61 Operational Training
Unit; early in 1943 she was
relegated to service at a
technical training school,
before finally being scrapped
in 1945.

Above: Henry Cozens pictured
as a Flight Lieutenant, in the
Royal Air Force officers'
full-dress uniform of the
1930s; note the small busby.
His career as a fighter pilot
began on Sopwith Snipes in
1923 and before he retired he
had flown Meteors and
Vampires.

During the summer of 1938 the first
Spitfires were issued to an RAF
squadron, No 19 at Duxford. Henry
Cozens commanded the Squadron then
and his account of the introduction of
the new high-performance monoplane
into service conveys well the mood in the
RAF — the finest flying club in the
world — at that time.

In December 1937 I was promoted to
Squadron Leader and posted to take
command of No 19 Squadron based at
Duxford near Cambridge. At that time
we flew the Gloster Gauntlet, a biplane
with an unimpressive performance
compared with the sort of opposition we
were likely to meet if it did come to a
war with Germany. I heard a buzz that
the first of the new Spitfire fighters were
to be issued to a squadron based at
Catterick in Yorkshire. I thought it
might be possible to change this, so I got
in touch with one of my friends at
Fighter Command headquarters and
asked him whether he thought the idea
of sending the first of these new fighters
so far north was sound. There was
bound to be a lot of Air Ministry interest
in the aircraft and Catterick was rather
a long way from London; and besides, it
was a notoriously small airfield. Might
not Duxford, a larger airfield much
closer to London, be more suitable? My
questions must have prompted the
correct line of thought because a few
weeks later I heard that my own
squadron, and No 66 which shared
Duxford with us, would be the first to
receive Spitfires.

On August 4th 1938, amid much
excitement, we received the first of the
new aircraft: Spitfire K 9789. I made
my first flight in her on the 11th. At that
time there were no pilots' notes on the
Spitfire, no conversion courses and, of
course, no dual control aircraft. I was
shown round the cockpit, given a
cheerful reminder to remember to
extend the undercarriage before I
landed, wished 'Good Luck', and off I
went.

After flying the Gauntlet, my first
impression of the Spitfire was that her
acceleration seemed rather slow and the
controls were a lot heavier than I had
expected. Thinking about it afterwards,
I realised why: the Gauntlet took off at
about 70mph and was flat-out at about
220mph; the Spitfire took off at about
the same speed but could do well over
350mph — in other words the speed
range was much greater, and although
the acceleration was in fact greater it
took somewhat longer to reach its
maximum speed. Moreover, as she
neared the top end of her speed range,
the Spitfire's controls became beauti-
fully light.

On August 16th I collected the second
of the Spitfires for Duxford, K 9792.
Nos 19 and 66 Squadrons were ordered
to carry out the intensive flying trials
using these two aircraft; our instructions
were to fly them both to 400 hours as
rapidly as possible and report our
findings. The two squadrons set about
the task with enthusiasm and the two
aircraft were airborne almost continuously from dawn to dusk; alone, I
amassed 24 flying hours in the Spitfire
before the end of August. We had a few
adventures. I remember one fine
afternoon seeing a Spitfire taxying in
and, as usual, the groundcrew were all
out watching her. Suddenly one of the
undercarriage legs started to fold. In no
time people were running towards the

aircraft from all directions and they grabbed the wing and managed to hold it up until the propeller stopped. The precious fighter escaped damage.

During these intensive flying trials Air Chief Marshal Sir Hugh Dowding, the C in C Fighter Command, visited us at Duxford. I showed him over the Spitfire and then we went to my office. When we were alone together he told me the position regarding this aircraft, it it came to a war. He said that the Hurricane was a great success and it could take on the Junkers 88 and the other German aircraft; but the Messerschmitt 109 was more than a match. So his question was: could the Spitfire take on the 109? If it could, then Fighter Command was prepared for war. If it could not, then we should have to think again.

As the intensive flying trial progressed I became convinced that the Spitfire could indeed take on the Messerschmitt 109 — and any other fighter then in existence. But that was not to say that she was perfect. For one thing the engines of these first Spitfires were difficult to start: the low-geared electric starter rotated the propeller blades so slowly that when a cylinder fired there was usually insufficient push to flick the engine round to fire the next; there would be a 'puff' noise, then the propeller would resume turning on the starter. Also, the early Merlin engines leaked oil terribly; it would run from the engine, down the fuselage and finally got blown away somewhere near the tail wheel. Yet another problem was what we called 'Spitfire Knuckle': when pumping up the undercarriage it was all too easy to rasp our knuckles on the side of the cockpit. There was a further problem for the taller pilots, who were always hitting their heads on the inside of the low cockpit canopy.

When we were about half way through the 400 hour trial I had a chat with Squadron Leader Fuller-Good who commanded 66 and we agreed that we had learned just about all we could from the exercise. I felt that if the First World War was anything to go by, no fighter was likely to last in action for anything like 400 hours. All we were now going

to find out was how to wear out two perfectly good Spitfires. So together we wrote an interim report on the new fighter and off it went. That set the wheels in motion and a few weeks later we received a high-powered deputation from the Air Ministry, Fighter Command Headquarters, Supermarine, Rolls Royce and Goodness knows where. We discussed the shortcomings at length and they promised to do what they could to overcome them. I remember that my own bandaged 'Spitfire Knuckle' made a particularly strong impression on the Supermarine team. The improvements we asked for were all incorporated in our own or later marks of the Spitfire. The simpler things like the bulged cockpit canopy to make life easier for the taller pilots and the faster starter motor, we received quite quickly. The improved oil seals for the Merlin took a little longer and leaking oil did remain

Top: First Spitfire write-off: on November 3rd 1938, with a total flying time of just over forty-one hours, K9792 ended her career at the close of Pilot Officer G. Sinclair's first flight in the type. The cause of the accident was a faulty axle stub which sheared during the landing. Sinclair was unhurt.

Above: Six of the original Spitfire pilots on No 19 Squadron: from left to right, Flying Officers Pace, Robinson, Clouston, Banham, Ball and, in the chair, Thomas.

Right: In an effort to reduce exhaust glare during night flying, Spitfire K9787 was tested with a new set of streamlined exhausts; although they were slightly better than the standard type, the improvement was not great enough to warrant production.

Far right: Press Day at Duxford, May 4th 1939 and for the first time No 19 Squadron was able to show off its new fighters on the the ground. By this time the squadron number on the fin has given way to the code-letters WZ on the fuselage and the white and yellow portions of the fuselage and above-wing roundels had been painted over in red and blue respectively. Other points of interest show up on this exceptionally clear Charles Brown photograph: the bead foresight for the guns, on the engine cowling mid-way between the pilot and the propeller; the protruding flash eliminators of the Browning guns; the bulged canopy hood on the third aircraft in line, contrasting with the flat early hood of the aircraft in front of it (this modification was not as some accounts have said to improve rearward visibility, but merely to allow greater headroom for the taller pilots); the undercarriage down indicator bar protruding from the top of the wing of the nearest aircraft; and the early type unarmoured windscreens and thin supporting masts for the radio aerials.

something of a problem throughout the Spitfire's service life. The later Mark I Spitfires had an engine-driven hydraulic system to raise and lower the undercarriage, which did away with the need to pump and resultant 'Spitfire Knuckle'.

During the early days we tried several different types of airscrew on the Spitfire. The original two-bladed fixed-pitch wooden propeller was designed to give its best performance at the high end of the performance envelope, but this produced serious disadvantages at the lower speeds; for example, during take-off it was almost stalled. We tried to get over this at first with a three-bladed propeller with a finer pitch, then with a three-bladed two-pitch propeller with one setting for take-off and another for high speed. I did not like the two-pitch propeller at all. It was far too easy to leave it in coarse pitch for take-off and that could give rise to a dangerous situation. There was no half-way house: the answer was the constant speed propeller, which automatically gave the correct pitch settings for all airspeeds. Early in 1939 I flew a trial with one of these and I remember being much impressed with the improvement in acceleration and general handling at low speeds. Fortunately, by the opening of the Battle of Britain, the operational Spitfires all had constant speed propellers.

Throughout the late summer and autumn of 1938 we received Spitfires at the rate of about one per week and the

Right: Spitfire I, Layout of cockpit.

Far right: The cockpit detail of one of the early production Mark I Spitfires; key:
1. Fixed Ring Gunsight.
2. Airspeed Indicator.
3. Artificial Horizon.
4. Rate of Climb and Descent Indicator.
5. Engine RPM Gauge.
6. Boost Gauge.
7. Fuel Pressure Gauge.
8. Oil Pressure Gauge.
9. Oil Temperature Gauge.
10. Radiator Temperature Gauge.
11. Directional Gyro.
12. Turn and Bank Indicator.
13 and 14. Fuel Contents Gauges.
15. 'Ki-gass' Fuel Priming Pump.
16. Priming Pump Selector Cock.
17. Fuel Cocks.
18. Gun Firing Button.
19. Tray for Magnetic Compass (compass not fitted to aircraft in photograph).
20. Hydraulic Handpump.
21. Undercarriage Position Selector.
22. Signalling Switch Box.
23. Control Column.
24. Rudder Pedals.

year was almost over before we were at our full strength of sixteen aircraft. Until we were up to strength and fully operational with Spitfires, we held on to our earlier Gauntlets and still flew them from time to time.

Jeffrey Quill, the Senior Test Pilot at Supermarine, was a frequent visitor to Duxford to see how we were getting on. One of the points he was a little anxious about was the size of the flaps on the Spitfire. Did we think they were too large for so light an aircraft? I agreed that they were a bit fierce, but I told him "Sooner or later people are going to hang things on this aircraft. I don't know what they will be, but I am certain that it will happen. And with the performance improvements planned by Supermarine the Spitfire is not going to get any *lighter,* is she?" He agreed that

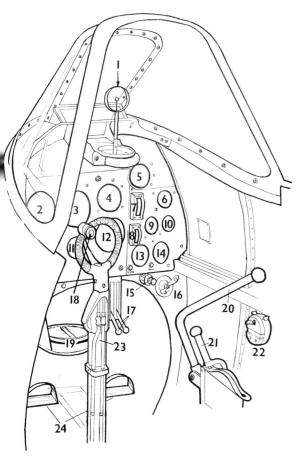

she would not, so we thought it better to leave the flaps alone and see what happened. As everybody now knows, the Spitfire more than doubled in weight during her development life; and to the very end the flaps were the same as they were in 1938.

When the Spitfires first arrived at Duxford they had lacked guns, but during the months that followed guns were fitted. I had my first experience of firing on November 3rd, at the range at Sutton Bridge; as it happened, it was a night sortie. I had expected a few sparks from each gun, but I was in no way prepared for the Brock's Benefit which came from each wing: the long tongues of flame lept out about ten feet in front of each gun. And the recoil of the eight fast-firing Brownings, after the two Vickers guns I had been used to in the Gauntlet, was unexpectedly severe; it slowed down the aircraft as though one had put the brakes on.

In January 1940 I left Duxford to take up a staff appointment. By then the Royal Air Force had more than a dozen squadrons fully equipped with the Spitfire, and several others were about to receive it. We on Nos 19 and 66 Squadrons had introduced the type into service and, I am proud to say, we did it without losing a man.

Below: Three new Spitfires pictured taking off from Eastleigh, at about the time of the outbreak of the Second World War. Up to September 3rd 1939 the Royal Air Force had accepted delivery of a total of 306 Spitfires, of which 187 formed the full equipment of ten squadrons (Nos 19, 41, 54, 65, 66, 72, 74, 602, 603 and 611) and part of the equipment of one more (No 609). A further 83 Spitfires were distributed as follows: at maintenance units, either in storage of for the fitting of operational equipment, 71; employed on trials at the makers or the various service test establishments, 11; and one had been allocated to a training unit. The remaining 36 Spitfires had been previously written-off in accidents.

First Encounter
Colonel Horst von Riesen

Spitfires of No 603 Squadron,
the first unit to achieve a kill
with the new fighter.

Above: Although the Spitfire pilots identified the enemy aircraft they engaged on October 16th 1939 as Heinkel 111s, they were in fact Junkers 88s like the one depicted here; during the action two of these bombers were shot down and others, including von Riesen's, suffered damage.

Right: Horst von Riesen who, as a young Leutnant, found himself confronted by Spitfires on the first day the new British fighter engaged the enemy: October 16th 1939.

On October 16th 1939 Spitfires of Nos 602 and 603 Squadrons took off to intercept a small force of German bombers attacking shipping in the Firth of Forth. For the first time, the new RAF fighter was to go into action against the enemy. Two of the German bombers were shot down, one of them being credited to Squadron Leader E. Stevens, the commander of No 603 Squadron. During the same engagement Pilot Officers Morton and Robertson, also of No 603 Squadron, reported intercepting an enemy aircraft 'thought to be an He111' over Rosyth and pursuing it out to sea at very low level. When they finally broke off their attacks the bomber's starboard engine was observed 'not running'. In fact the German bombers involved in the day's

attack on the Firth of Forth were not Heinkel 111s, as was widely reported in British accounts of the action, but Junkers 88s. And Horst von Riesen should know — because he was one of those on the receiving end!

In the autumn of 1939 I was a young Leutnant serving with the First *Gruppe* of *Kampfgeschwader 30,* based at Westerland on the island of Sylt. At that time we were the only unit in the *Luftwaffe* to be equipped with our fast new long range dive-bomber — the Junkers 88.

Initially our activities had kept us well clear of the British defences. But on the morning of October 16th one of our reconnaissance aircraft spotted the battlecruiser *HMS Hood* entering the Firth of Forth. We received orders to attack her, if we could catch her in open water; but at that stage of the war both sides tried hard to avoid causing civilian casualties and we had the strictest orders that if she was in harbour we were either to attack other warships outside, or else return with our bombs.

Nine of our aircraft were bombed-up and took off, but when we arrived over Rosyth we found Hood safely in dock — where we were not allowed to harm her. Just to the east of the Forth Bridge there were some small warships, however, and

24

I decided to attack one of these. I selected one and carried out a diving attack, but scored only a near-miss.

Then, as I was climbing away, my radio operator suddenly shouted over the intercom that there were several fighters about two kilometres away, diving on us. I looked in the direction he was pointing and as soon as I saw them I knew that I would need all the speed I could possibly squeeze out of my Junkers if we were to escape. I pushed down the nose and, throttles wide open, dived for the sea. But it was no good. The Spitfires, as we soon recognized them to be, had had the advantage of speed and height from the start and they soon caught up with us. As I sped down the Firth of Forth just a few metres above the surface, I could see clearly the splashes from the shells from the shore batteries, as they too joined in the unequal battle.

Now I thought I was finished. Guns were firing at me from all sides, and the Spitfires behind seemed to be taking turns at attacking. But I think my speed gave them all a bit of a surprise — I was doing more than 400 kilometres per hour (250mph), which must have been somewhat faster than any other bomber they had trained against at low level — and of course I jinked from side to side to make their aim as difficult as possible. At one stage in the pursuit I remember looking down and seeing what looked like rain drops hitting the water. It was all very strange. Then I realised what it was: those splashes marked the impact of bullets being aimed at me from above!

I had only one ally: time. Every minute longer the Junkers kept going meant another seven kilometres further out to sea and further from the Spitfires' base; and I had far more fuel to play with than they did. Finally, however, the inevitable happened: after a chase of more than twenty minutes there was a sudden 'phooff' and my starboard motor suddenly disappeared from view in a cloud of steam. One of the enemy bullets had pierced the radiator, releasing the vital coolant and without it the motor was finished. There was no alternative but to shut it down before it burst into flames.

My speed sagged to 180kph (112mph) — almost on the stall when flying asymmetric — and we were only a few metres above the waves. Now the Junkers was a lame duck. But when I looked round, expecting to see the Spitfires curving in to finish us off, there was no sign of them. They had turned round and gone home.

Even so, we were in a difficult position. With that airspeed there lay

Below: Spitfire Is of No 74 Squadron, pictured at Hornchurch early in 1940. The second Spitfire in the line would appear to be a new arrival, because her squadron letters had not yet been painted on.

Above, Right: With friends like that who needs enemies? Flight Lieutenant Wilfred Clouston of No 19 Squadron standing beside his aircraft as she lay on Newmarket racecourse, following an adventurous flight on March 4th 1940. He had been leading his section in a line astern formation when his No 2 collided with his tail and the propeller slashed away most of his tail control surfaces; skilfully he belly-landed the Spitfire, without incurring further major damage. Clouston displayed similar flying ability during the Battle of Britain, in which he was credited with twelve victories.

Right: An historic photograph: taken at Le Bourget airport, Paris, on May 16th 1940, it shows the Flamingo airliner which took Mr Churchill to discuss with the French premier the provision of the Royal Air Force fighters for the Battle of France. In the background may be seen the Spitfires of Blue Section of No 92 Squadron, which provided the escort.

ahead of us a flight of nearly four hours, if we were to get back to Westerland. During our training we had been told that a Ju 88 would not maintain height on one engine — and we were only barely doing so. Should we ditch there and then? I thought no; it was getting dark, nobody would pick us up and we would certainly drown or die of exposure. An alternative was to turn round and go back to Scotland, and crash land there. One of my crew suggested this but one of the others — I don't know who — shouted over the intercom 'No, no, never! If we go back there the Spitfires will certainly get us!' He was right. The thought of going back into that hornets' nest horrified us. So we decided to carry on as we were and see what happened. We prefered to risk death from drowing or the cold, rather than have to face those Spitfires again.

Gradually, as we burnt our fuel and the aircraft became lighter, I was able to coax the Junkers a little higher. The remaining motor, though pressed to the limit, continued running and finally we did get back to Westerland.

So it was that I survived my first encounter with Spitfires. I would meet them again during the Battle of Britain, over the Mediterranean and during the Battle of Sicily. It was not a pleasant experience.

Aces to be: Blue Section of No 92 Squadron, pictured in May 1940; from left to right, Pilot Officer Bob Holland (later credited with 13 victories), Flying Officer Robert Stanford-Tuck (later 29 victories) and Pilot Officer Alan Wright (later 10 victories). All three opened their scores while covering the Dunkirk evacuation. Beneath the open hood of the Spitfire in the background, it is just possible to make out the GR code letters carried by No 92 Squadron's aircraft for a short period early in the war.

GENERAL COMBAT REPORT   May 25th 1940

No 92 Squadron while on patrol Boulogne—Calais—Dunkirk from 1720 to 1920 hours sighted a large formation of enemy aircarft over Calais at 8-10,000ft. About 30 enemy aircraft, mostly ME 110s, were ahead and behind them a further group of 15-20 aircaraft of types not identified, but including Ju 87s and Ju 88s. Some aircraft started dive-bombing attacks on Boulogne harbour, with others circling in the vicinity. No 92 Squadron at 4,000ft climbed to engage and a series of dog fights ensued, mainly with Me 110s. Blue 1 states that he saw some Hurricanes already engaging the enemy, but as the sky was so full of aircraft a clear statement of the situation is impossible. As a result of the dogfight 7 Me 110s were definitely shot down, 5 Me 110s and 2 Ju 88s probably shot down. Most of our aircraft were hit many times.

Pilots state that the Me 110 evasive tactics are a steep turn towards the Spitfire's tail, to enable the rear gunner to open fire.

About 20 Me 110s were seen flying in line astern in a right circle round the bombers, which was very difficult to attack. The Me 110 is not so fast as the Spitfire on the level, but very good in a fast turn and a steep dive, though the Spitfire can hold it on a turn. They appear to use the stall turn a great deal.

Enemy camouflage standard.

During the first two minutes of the combat, a continuous transmission in German was heard on the R/T.

The following is an assessment of the aircraft shot down by the pilots:

	Certain	Possible
F/Lt Tuck	1 Me 110	1 Me 110
P/O Holland	2 Me 110	1 Ju 88
P/O Wright	1 Me 110	—
P/O Williams	1 Me 110	1 Me 110
Sgt Havercroft	—	1 Me 110
P/O Edwards	—	1 Ju 88
Sgt Barraclough	—	1 Me 110
P/O Bartley	2 Me 110	—

Sqn Ldr Bushell, F/Lt Gillies and Sgt Klipsche are missing (one Spitfire was seen to crash to the ground). F/Lt Green landed at Hawkinge with a bullet wound in his leg.

An Even Match

During the early war period, from September 1939 to May 1940, the Spitfire squadrons all remained in Britain and had no opportunity to go into action against their opposite numbers in the *Luftwaffe*. The lull in the west came to an abrupt halt on May 10th, however, when the Germans launched their great offensive into Holland, Belgium and France. Soon there was no need for the Spitfire squadrons to go overseas to new bases in order to meet the enemy; instead, the land battle was being fought on territory within even their limited radius of action from airfields in south-eastern England. From May 12th, when No 66 Squadron's Spitfires mounted a patrol over The Hague, the new fighter was committed to action in steadily greater numbers. At last the Spitfire was to come face-to-face with its *Luftwaffe* equivalent — the Messerschmitt 109E.

The initial encounters between these two adversaries were usually inconclusive, though they did demonstrate that they were obviously closely comparable in performance. Also during May 1940, however, in the still-peaceful skies over the Royal Aircraft Establishment at Farnborough, a Spitfire I and a captured Messerschmitt 109E fought a series of mock combats as part of a trial intended to determine the strengths and weaknesses of each compared with the other.

To provide a fair picture of the capability of each aircraft, they were flown in pre-planned tactical exercises. In the first of these, flown at 6,000 feet, the Messerschmitt was positioned ahead of the Spitfire and its pilot attempted to shake off his pursuer by means of a horizontal speed run, three of four tight turns in each direction, a dive, then a steep climb; afterwards the two aircraft changed positions and repeated the procedure, then engaged in a short free-play fight.

In level flight, the maximum speeds of the two aircraft were about equal. During the turns, flown at speeds between 90 and 220mph, the Spitfire had little difficulty in keeping behind; nor did the dive present the pursuer with any great problem. When the Messerschmitt was pulled out of the dive and into a steep climb at low airspeed, however, the Spitfire — whose optimum climb rate was achieved at a flatter angle but a higher airspeed — had difficulty in following; and even when she could follow, the pilots found it almost impossible to hold their gunsight on the target.

When the Spitfire was in front, it was clear that in a turning match at medium altitude and in the middle of her speed range, she was easily the better aircraft; also, with her superior rate of roll, she could shake off her pursuer by means of a flick half-roll and quick pull out of the

Below: A Spitfire I of No 54 Squadron, flown by Pilot Officer Colin Gray; this aircraft was one of the first to be fitted with the constant speed propeller which greatly improved performance.

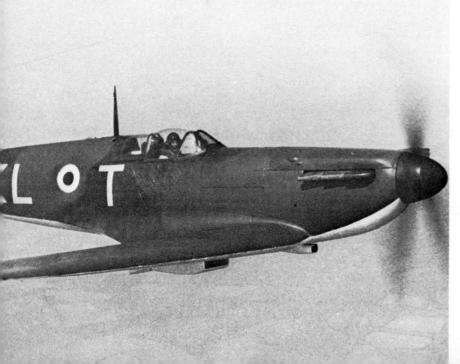

subsequent dive. The Messerschmitt pilot found the latter particularly difficult to counter, because when he rolled after the Spitfires his speed built up rapidly in the steep dive and his elevator became so heavy that a quick pull out was impossible. Of course, these advantages could be exploited only if the Spitfire was flown to her limits; during subsequent trial flights there were several occasions when the Messerschmitt succeeded in remaining on the tail of the Spitfire merely because the latter's pilot lacked experience and failed to tighten his turn sufficiently, for fear of stalling and spinning.

Manoeuverability at medium speeds is only one of many factors which can be turned to advantage in an air combat, however, and two points emerged from the trial whose significance was to be confirmed again and again during the great air battles soon to follow. The first was that if the Messerschmitt pilot pushed his aircraft into a sudden bunt and the Spitfire tried to follow, the latter's engine would splutter and stop because the normal float-type carburettor fitted to the Merlin ceased to deliver fuel; the Messerschmitt's Daimler Benz engine had direct fuel injection and did not suffer from this failing (later, Spitfire pilots learned to half-roll and pull down when following bunting Messerschmitt 109s, using an aileron turn to get back upright when they were established in the dive. It was not an ideal solution, but it did enable a

good pilot to maintain the pursuit). The second point was that during diving manoeuvers at high speeds the controls, and particularly the ailerons, of both aircraft became progressively heavier; at 400mph the Spitfire's rate of roll was about the same as that of the Messerschmitt 109, with both pilots having to pull as hard as they could on the stick to get one-fifth aileron movement and both aircraft requiring about four seconds to roll through 45 degrees. Under these conditions the Spitfire ceased to have any clear advantage in manoeuverability and, as German fighter pilots soon discovered in combat, so long as they kept their speed up and evaded the Spitfire pilot would find it hard to bring his guns to bear.

One important lesson failed to emerge from the Farnborough trial: the general superiority of the German fighter at altitudes above 20,000 feet. Before the war, and during its early stages, many experts in Britain considered high altitude dogfighting to be so unlikely as not to warrant a trial; they would shortly learn otherwise.

Overall, however, the Spitfire I and the Messerschmitt 109E matched each other fairly evenly. If they fought, victory would almost invariably go to the side which was the more alert, which held the initiative, which understood the strengths and weaknesses of its opponents aircraft, which showed the better team work and which, in the last resort, could shoot the more accurately.

Below: The Messerschmitt 109E, which equipped virtually the whole of the German single-engined fighter force throughout 1940.

Battle of Britain

This Spitfire of No 92
Squadron crash-landed at
Biggin Hill in September
1940. Note the wheel and
undercarriage leg lying on
the grass just behind the
aircraft.

Left: Pilots of No 92 Squadron at readiness at Bibury, during the Battle of Britain. On the left is Flight Lieutenant Charles Kingcombe, one of the unit's top scorers, who during the battle was credited with three enemy aircraft destroyed, four probably destroyed and eight damaged. The pilot with his back to the camera is wearing a captured German life jacket, a trophy with few advantages over its British counterpart.

Left: Illustrating the mixed origins of the men who fought in the Battle of Britain are these four officers of No 19 Squadron pictured at Fowlmere: from left to right, Pilot Officer W. 'Jock' Cunningham, from Glasgow; Sub Lieutenant 'Admiral' Blake, a Fleet Air Arm pilot on loan to the RAF; Flight Lieutenant F. Dolezal, a Czech who had been in his own country's air force before the Germans took over, who had escaped and joined the French Air Force, escaped again and was now with the RAF; Flying Officer F. Brinsden, a New Zealander. Blake was killed in action right at the end of the battle, on October 29th, when his Spitfire was shot down by a Messerschmitt 109.

Above: Flying Officer 'Uncle Sam' Leckrone, an American volunteer, fought during the Battle with Nos 616 and 19 Squadrons; he later became a founder member of No 71, the first 'Eagle' Squadron.

Left: Groundcrewmen clustered round a Spitfire of No 92 Squadron during a rapid turn round, probably at Biggin Hill in September 1940.

Right: During a fight with Messerschmitt 109s on August 9th, Sergeant H. Mann of No 64 Squadron had a cannon shell jam his control column; he managed to land his Spitfire, albeit heavily, at Kenley.

Top: Pilot Officer Alan Wright of No 92 Squadron suffered hits to his aircraft during a fight with Messerschmitts on September 9th; one 7.9mm bullet fired from behind passed through his perspex hood, nicked the windscreen frame near the top, bounced off the toughened glass windscreen and smashed his reflector sight; Wright himself escaped injury.

Above: During a head-on confrontation with a Messerschmitt in September, Pilot Officer C. Bodie of No 66 Squadron had his toughened glass windscreen put to the test.

Right: Throughout the battle, gas attack on the Fighter Command airfields was an ever-present threat. Accordingly the ground crews always kept their gas masks and anti-gas capes close at hand—though rarely as close as this posed photograph might suggest. In the cockpit is Flight Lieutenant K. M. Gillies, the commander of 'A' Flight of No 66 Squadron; he was killed in action on October 4th.

Left: Members of the Luftwaffe examining a Spitfire of No 234 Squadron which had landed near near Cherbourg on August 15th, after suffering damage during an air battle over mid-Channel. Examination of other German photographs of the hole to the rear of the cockpit reveals that the plating had been blown outwards, almost certainly by the explosion of the destructor charge carried to demolish the secret IFF equipment. Note also the holed canopy, and the half-completed Luftwaffe cross on the fuselage.

Below: This picture of a burning Spitfire rolling past an He 111 appeared in a German aviation periodical shortly after the Battle of Britain.

Bob Oxspring was one of the few who fought in Fighter Command for control of the skies over Britain, during the fatefull summer of 1940. In this section he describes the action he is least likely to forget.

October 25th 1940; the Battle of Britain was in its closing stages, though at the time we had no way of knowing that this was the case. I was a very new Flight Lieutenant on No 66 Squadron, then based at Gravesend. Soon after breakfast we were scrambled and I was ordered to take my Flight of six Spitfires to patrol over Maidstone at 30,000 feet; the Germans were putting in the occasional fighter sweep and fighter-bomber attack and it was one of these we were after. When we arrived over Maidstone there was nothing to be seen, however; from the ground we received further orders to orbit overhead and wait.

It was nearly half an hour later that the 'bandits' did show up: six Messerschmitt 109s. For once we had a perfect set-up: we were up-sun, we had a 2,000 foot drop on them and the numbers were exactly equal. It did not often turn out like that during the Battle of Britain. I told my pilots to take one each and down we went. But the Germans were wide awake and I watched my man, the leader, suddenly barrel round and pull his fighter into a steep dive. I had been half expecting it and I tore down after him almost vertically, gaining slowly but surely. I had him cold. It never occured to me to watch my own tail — after all, we had covered all six of the Messerschmitts. Well, confidence is that nice warm feeling you have just before you slide over the banana skin. I was in range and just about to open fire when, suddenly, my Spitfire shuddered under the impact of a series of explosions. In fact those six Messerschmitts had been covering a seventh, a decoy aircraft a couple of thousand feet beneath them; their idea had been to bounce any of our fighters

A Day to Remember
Group Captain Bob Oxspring, DFC and two bars, AFC

having a go at it. And the German leader had taken me right in front of the decoy, who got in a good squirt at me as I went past.

He must have hit my elevator controls, because the next thing I knew my Spitfire was pulling uncontrollably up into a tight loop; a loop so tight that the 'G' forces squeezed me hard into my seat and blacked me out. As I went down the other side of the loop the aircraft straightened out and I could see again, but as the speed built up the jammed elevators took effect and up we went into a second loop. Obviously the time had come for me to part company with that Spitfire. But first I had to get the hood open and that was not proving easy: the only time I could reach up and see to do it was when the 'G' was off; but then we were screaming downhill fast and the hood would not budge. I thought my time had come and I remember thinking of the injustice of it all: hit just as I was about to blow that Messerschmitt out of the sky!

I have no idea how many loops the Spitfire did before I was finally able to slide back the hood. But it was not a moment too soon, because by then the oil tank was on fire and the flames were spreading back from the engine. I threw off my seat harness and stood up, but found I could go no further because I still had my helmet on and it was attached firmly to the aircraft. By now I was getting pretty desperate and I wrenched the helmet off with all my strength. Afterwards I found the helmet in the wreckage and saw that I had actually torn it across the leather; I was amazed at the force I must have summoned to do that.

The next thing I knew I was falling clear of my aircraft, head-down and on my back, at an angle of about forty-five degrees. I had no idea how high I was, so I pulled the D-ring right away. I knew it was a mistake, as soon as I did it.

When the parachute began to deploy, I was in just about the worst possible position. I remember watching, an interested spectator, as the canopy and the rigging lines came streaming out from between my legs. One of the lines

coiled itself round my leg and when the canopy developed I found myself hanging upside down. I had never parachuted before, but from my sketchy previous instruction I was fairly certain that head-first was not the position to be in when I hit the ground! So I grabbed a handful of slack rigging lines on the opposite side to my entangled leg and started to climb up hand over hand. After a lot of kicking and pulling I managed to get my leg free; with a sigh of relief I sank back into my harness, right way up.

Now I had time to think about what was happening around me. The first thing that struck me was the quietness; the only sounds were the spasmodic bursts of cannon and machine-gun fire and the howls of the engines, coming from the battle still in progress high above; it seemed an age since I had been part of it. But my own troubles were not over yet.

Gradually it began to dawn on me that the straps leading up from my harness, instead of being comfortably clear of my head on either side, were tangled together and chafing my ears and face. And higher up the rigging lines were also tangled, preventing the canopy from developing to its fullest extent. That meant that I was falling much faster than I should have been; and

Right: The winter of 1940-1941: up at Oh-God-Zero-Zero, ready and waiting for the enemy that seemed no longer to come. Dawn readiness at Biggin Hill; from left to right Sergeant J. Le Cheminant, Pilot Officer Sam Saunders and Pilot Officer Morris, all of No 92 Squadron.

struggle as I might, I could not get the lines untangled. I went down past a cloud and it seemed to whizz by: it was not going to be a very pleasant landing. The only time I had ever needed a parachute and this had to happen!

Gradually I got lower, and I could make out trees and farm houses and curious faces raised skywards. At about 500 feet the wind carried me across some high tension cables and even though I was hundreds of feet above the wires I could not resist the instinct to lift my feet up. Still I was coming down much too fast. The one thing I needed most of all was a nice soft tree, to break my fall. And there in my line of drift, in answer to my prayer, was a wood full of them.

Just before I hit I covered my face with my arms and came to rest amid the crack of breaking twigs. When the noise stopped I cautiously lowered my arms and looked around. My parachute canopy was draped across a couple of trees and I was bouncing up and down between the trunks like a yo-yo. I was about twenty feet up, suspended above an asphalt road.

At about my level, just out of reach, was a small branch. By doing a sort of Tarzan stunt, swinging back and forth from side to side, I was able to get closer and closer until in the end I was able to grab hold of it. Gingerly I pulled myself

up and on to a thicker bough, before letting go of my harness. By this time quite a crowd had begun to collect underneath the tree; at first there seemed to be some doubt about my nationality but the vehemence of my Anglo-Saxon demands for help soon satisfied everyone that I was, in fact, British. Some Home Guard men made a human ladder by sitting on each others' shoulders and with their aid I managed to clamber down to mother earth. It had indeed been a memorable day.

Above: Bob Oxspring, pictured earlier in the war prior to a high altitude patrol, wearing the fleece-lined leather flying jacket and trousers issued to pilots. The jackets were popular; but the trousers were too cumbersome and restricted movement and were rarely worn by Spitfire pilots going into action.

Right: Fred Tandy, pictured in 1940 when he served on No 616 Squadron.

Below: Armourers at Duxford re-arming a Spitfire of No 19 Squadron in September 1940. Note that the fabric patches covering the gun ports have been blown off, indicating that the guns had been fired. The armourers under the near wing have just removed two of the used ammunition boxes and are in the process of removing the other two.

Feeding the Guns
Warrant Officer Fred Tandy, BEM

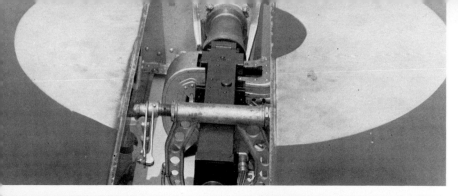

through the breech of the gun; this was important, because it meant that we could now re-arm the Spitfire without having to remove the top covers from the gun bays. As a result of continual practice, and with twelve covers to remove instead of the original twenty, we cut the original twenty-minute re-arming time down by more than half.

By the time of the Battle of Britain, re-arming had become a slick operation. As the Spitfire taxied in after its sortie, we armourers would be watching the canvas strips doped over the gun ports: if these had been blown off it meant the guns had been fired and re-arming was necessary. If this was the case and the aircraft was required to fly again immediately, the team of armourers would be waiting at the dispersal. Each man carried one ammunition box loaded with 300 rounds of .303" ammunition under each arm. During

Nobody who worked on the Spitfire's guns will ever forget the knuckle-rasping hand-slashing experience of having to feel one's way round the cramped gun bays with their sharp edges and numerous pieces of locking wire.

Top: A .303" Browning installation from behind and above, with the upper panel removed. The rear stirrup with the screw for left-right harmonisation can be seen holding the rear of the gun.

Above: The installation from behind and below; to the left of the gun may be seen the harmonisation locking quadrant for raising or lowering the barrel; the braided cable running underneath the gun carried high pressure air to fire the weapon.

To operate effectively, those who fly are utterly dependant upon the skill, determination and enthusiasm of those who prepare and repair their aircraft. Representing those men who played such an essential part in winning the Battle of Britain, yet who never left the ground, is Fred Tandy. An armourer, his task during the battle was to ensure that when a pilot had the enemy in his sights and pressed the firing button, the battery of guns performed the final act in the long chain of events between the order to take-off and the destruction of an enemy. In this section he recounts the re-arming of the Spitfire's eight Browning guns.

I joined No 616 Squadron with Spitfire Is at Leconfield in January 1940, as an AC 1 armourer straight out of training. We were young and very keen and whenever there was an aircraft available we used to practice re-arming again and again to try to reduce the time needed. Initially it took a team of four armourers about twenty minutes to carry out this task. Then somebody worked out a way of using a canvas loop to pull the first round of the new ammunition belt

the Battle it was usual to load two of the guns with armour-piercing ammunition, two with incendiary and four guns with ball ammunition; four out of the last 25 rounds in each box of ball ammunition were tracer, to give the pilot an indication that he was nearly out.

Even before the propellor had stopped there would be two armourers under each wing, busily undoing the scores of half-turn Dzus fasteners securing the gun panels and the ammunition box covers. Once these covers were off, the next step was to have a quick look into the breech mechanism of each gun, to check that there had been no stoppage and that the gun was serviceable: if the breech block was stopped in the rear position, it meant that the pilot had ceased fire; if it was stopped in the forward position, it meant that he had run out of ammunition; if there had been a stoppage the breech would usually be in the forward position, with a live round 'up the spout'.

Unless the gun was unserviceable, the breech mechanism would be pulled to the rear position if it was not there already; then the belts from the used ammunition boxes could be pulled clear, and the boxes themselves could be removed and placed on the ground out of the way. Now the guns were safe and one armourer on each side would start to swab out the gun barrels from the front, to clean away the crumbs of burnt cordite; for this he would use a cleaning rod, with first a piece of oily and then a piece of clean 'four-by-two' flannel. Meanwhile the second armourer in the pair would be clicking the full ammunition boxes into place from underneath the wing, and threading the canvas straps round the first round in each one through the feed ways. With a firm pull on each one in turn, he would bring the first round in each new box up

Below: Cartridge cases and belt links spewing out of the underwing chutes of a Spitfire, probably one belonging to No 602 Squadron, during the simultaneous firing of all eight Brownings at the butts. Almost certainly this firing was set up specially for the benefit of press cameramen, for it formed no part of the normal Spitfire checking procedure. If the servicability of a gun was suspect, it was removed and fired individually. An interesting point to note on this photograph, however, is the horizontal strake running along the upper fuselage just in front of the cockpit; it was a local modification to enable a light alloy screen to be fitted to shield the pilot's eyes from the glare of the exhaust flames during night flying.

against the feed stops. Then he would cock the gun using either the special wire cocking tool or, more usually, his forage cap. Cocking brought the first round out of the belt on to the face of the breech block and at the same time released the canvas loop which could then be pulled clear. The armourer would look up into the gun from underneath to check that the round had actually fed on to the face of the breech block, then press the manual release to bring the block forwards to feed the round into the chamber; the rear-sear-retainer-keeper would hold the firing pin clear of the round, so there was no risk of the gun going off at this stage. But I would point out that it was considered very bad manners if you carried out this stage of the re-arming process, while the other fellow was still working on the gun barrel from the front!

Now, the only essential task remaining was to re-fit the gun and ammunition box covers to the underside of the wing. If there was time before the next take-off we would dope pieces of fabric over the firing ports, to keep the heat in and prevent the guns freezing up at high altitude; to save time during the Battle of Britain, we sometimes used ordinary medical sticking plaster for this purpose. If the grass was wet the Spitfire was notorious for throwing up mud and water on to the undersides of the wings during the take-off run; to prevent this moisture getting into the gun bays via the link and cartridge case ejector slots, we would dope pieces of newspaper over them.

At the end of a day's fighting we would take the recoils out of the guns and clean them properly; or, if the Spitfire had been stood down from immediate readiness to, say, 30 minutes, we would remove one recoil mechanism at a time for cleaning.

On the Spitfire our responsibilities as armourers did not end with the guns. Each morning we had to change the 'colours of the day' in the Plessey six-barrelled signal cartridge discharger. And each time the guns were fired we had to fit a new film magazine into the

G42 cine-camera located in the port wing root. Finally we had to check for security the two 4 inch diameter parachute flares fitted in their long chutes just behind the cockpit; these were sometimes used during night flying.

In 1940 there was a tremendous sense of 'belonging' to one's fighter squadron. Three ground crewmen were allocated to each Spitfire: a fitter, a rigger and an armourer; and it was a matter of great distress if anything happened to 'their' pilot. Yet in spite of quite severe losses in pilots, morale was sky-high. At Kenley during the Battle of Britain we could see the combats being fought overhead; we could see the enemy aircraft being shot down and we knew that we on the ground had our own vital part to play in bringing this about. For a young lad of nineteen, they were stirring times.

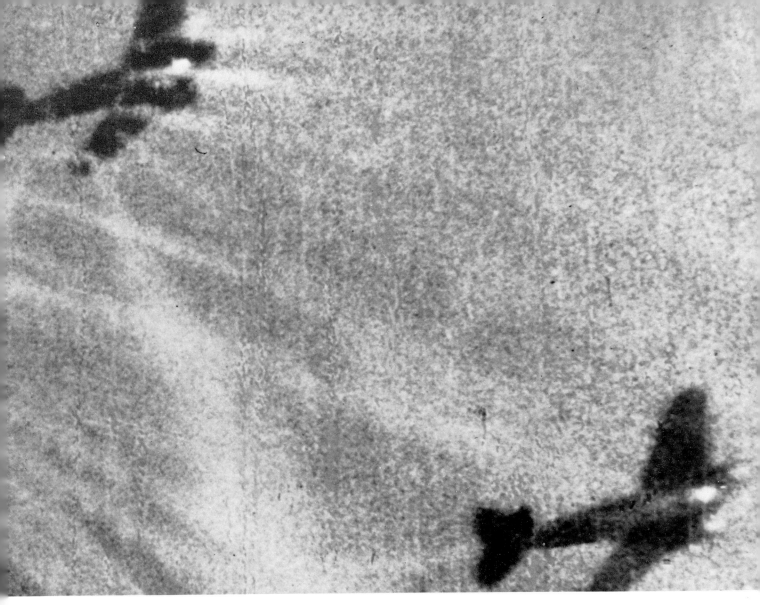

Left: An answer to the problem: the 20mm Hispano cannon. Seen here is the prototype installation of this weapon in a Spitfire I, serial L1007, in June 1939. During the early stages of the Battle of Britain No 19 Squadron flew cannon-armed Spitfires in action; but in its early form the 20mm Hispano installation proved unreliable and was the subject of frequent stoppages. The aircraft fitted with it had to be withdrawn from operations pending modifications. By the end of 1940 the bugs had been ironed out and the cannon-armed Spitfire entered general service. Fired from short range the 20mm solid round could defeat the thickest armour carried by the German medium bombers; hits near the fuel tanks with the 20mm high explosive round stood a good chance of causing petrol leaks which the self sealing was quite unable to staunch.

Above: Enough to make the difference: the small amount of sweep-up shown, on the tail-plane trailing edge of Spitfire P7525, was sufficient to spoil the airflow over the rudder and elevators; this limited her diving speed to 320mph 1AS and produced an uncomfortable left yaw.

Sorting Out a Rogue

18th January 1941.
Aeroplane and Armament Experimental Establishment Boscombe Down. Spitfire II P 7525 (66 Squadron): Handling and Diving Trials.

Small defects in an airframe, defects not readily apparent to the eye, can cause unusual handling characteristics in the air. When that happened to Spitfires and all the normal cures had been tried and had failed, the experts at Boscombe Down were called in to try to find out what was wrong. This report illustrates how they cured the poor handling characteristics found on Spitfire P 7525. The report was written early in 1941. Yet even before it began to be circulated it had ceased to be of relevant interest so far as P 7525 was concerned: almost immediately after the Spitfire had been put right and returned to No 66 Squadron, she was written off in a crash after running out of fuel in bad weather.

1.0 Introduction.

Complaints were made by No 66 Squadron that the handling qualities of this aeroplane, which was representative of others in the Squadron, were bad because in spite of full forward trim the aeroplane could not be dived to more than 320mph IAS. Also, it was very left wing low in the dive and there was insufficient rudder bias to prevent it from yawing to the left. There was a considerable amount of aileron snatch which was also a subject of complaint.

2.0 Tests carried out

2.1 The aeroplane was flown as received and the Squadron's criticisms confirmed. It was check weighed and the centre of gravity determined; also the range of trimmer movement was checked. These measurements confirmed that the aeroplane was a normal Spitfire II so far as these points were concerned. Examination of the fin and tail plane trailing edges showed that they were swept up sufficiently to spoil the flow over the rudder and elevator and the respective trimmers. The

Above: On finals for landing, after a curved approach to enable the pilot to keep the airfield in sight. Hood locked open . . . side door on half-cock position (to prevent any possibility of the hood slamming shut in the event of a mishap) . . . break-pressure checked . . . undercarriage down (below 160mph), two green lights and indicator bars out . . . mixture rich . . . pitch lever to fully fine . . . flaps down (below 140mph) . . . over the hedge at 85mph indicated . . . ease the stick gently back to hold her off the ground as the speed falls away . . . 64mph indicated and she stalls gently on to the ground.

attached photograph shows this clearly.

2.2 The trailing edges of the fin and tail plane were dressed down until the sweep up was removed. In addition, the 8″ and 6″ lengths of under standard-size trimming cord doped to the upper port and lower starboard aileron trailing edges respectively were removed and a single 10″ length of full size cord was doped to the upper trailing edge of the port aileron*. A certain amount of the backlash present in the aileron circuit was absorbed by tightening the cables but the remainder could not be eliminated readily, because it was due to a little slackness in the hinge pins.

2.3 After these alterations the aeroplane was flown to check the handling and diving qualities. It was trimmed for full throttle level flight, the elevator trimmer indicator then being at the normal setting of 1½ to 1¼ divisions nose down and dived up to the limiting speed of 460mph IAS. No abnormal forward pressure was required on the control column and neither yaw nor wing dropping was experienced in the dive when the normal amount of starboard bias was used. The ailerons were found to be slightly overbalanced, until at about 440mph IAS the over-balancing and snatching became disconcerting. This snatching was very apparent in tight turns and to a lesser degree when pulling out of the dives.

3.0 Conclusions

3.1 The modifications carried out on the aeroplane restored its handling qualities to normal and made it representative of other Mark II Spitfires, with the exception of the aileron control.

3.2 The trailing edges of all fin and tailplane surfaces of Spitfire aeroplanes should be carefully inspected to ensure that the contours are not distorted.

3.3 Aileron hing pins should have just sufficient clearance to eliminate mechanical stiffness; the control cables should be kept taut.

*On the early Spitfires fitted with fabric-covered ailerons, lengths of cord were doped on the ailerons to trim the aircraft to fly 'hands off' in the rolling plane. On later aircraft with metal-covered ailerons, trim was achieved by bending them.

47

Spitfire Vs of the second
Norwegian fighter squadron
to form in Britain, No 332,
pictured at Catterick.

Circus 62

By the end of 1940 the Luftwaffe had had to cease its large scale daylight operatons over Britain, as the bulk of its combat units began moving eastwards for the planned invasion of Russia. Relieved of the need to defend Britain against massed air attacks the new C in C Fighter Command, Air Chief Marshal Sir Sholto Douglas, adopted a policy he termed 'leaning forward into France'.

From the beginning of 1941 Fighter Command flew offensive sweeps over the northern fringes of occupied Europe. The German invasion of Russia, in June, provided an added driving force for these operations: anything the British forces could now do, to divert German forces away from the eastern front, was of great importance.

The 'Circus' was the largest of the routine offensive air operations mounted over northern Europe during 1941. We shall now examine one of these in detail: No 62, which took place on Thursday, August 7th.

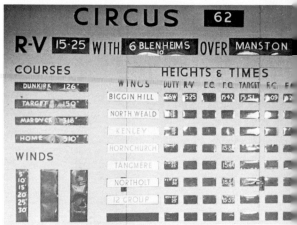

Above: "That's where you're going . . . " Squadron Leader 'Spy' de la Torre, the station Intelligence officer, points out the route of Circus 62 soon after it had been marked up in the briefing room at Biggin Hill on August 7th 1941. The concentration of parallel lines shows the route of the bombers and their escorting wings to and from Lille. The less distinct lines from the west show the planned routes of the Tangmere and Hornchurch Wings into the target area.

Right: The briefing board at Biggin Hill on August 7th 1941, being prepared for the briefing of pilots prior to Circus 62. The board shows the duties of each of the fighter wings taking part in the operation; when completed it will show each one's time to rendezvous with the bombers (if applicable) and the times for each wing to be at the English coast, the French coast and the target.

The object of the Circus operation was to use a small force of RAF bombers as bait, to lure up the German fighters which could then be engaged by the large covering force of RAF fighters. The ground target for Circus 62 was the power station at Lille and six Blenheim bombers of No 2 Group were to attack it. In its composition the Circus forces could be likened to a lot of froth but very little beer. The 'beer', the force of six bombers, was covered by a mass of 'froth': no fewer than eighteen squadrons of Spitfires and two squadrons of Hurricanes, to provide escort and support during the various phases of the action.

Late on the afternoon of the 7th the bombers joined up with their escorting fighters over Manston and headed south-eastwards towards their target. As the close-cover fighter squadrons slid into their briefed positions, this part of the force took on a recognisable shape. With the bombers at 12,000 feet flew the Spitfires of No 71 (US Eagle) Squadron; behind and 1,000 feet above them came those of No 111; and behind and a further 1,000 feet above came the Spitfires of No 222 Squadron. These three squadrons, all from North Weald, comprised the escort wing. Similarly stepped up behind and above came three more Spitfire squadrons, Nos 452 (Australian), 485 (New Zealand) and 602 Squadrons from Kenley, making up the escort cover wing.

These six squadrons of fighters and one of bombers formed the hub of aerial activity, around which the supporting wings of fighters centred their activity. Planned in great detail, the Circus was indeed a far cry from the hasty defensive scrambles of the Battle of Britain just a few months earlier; now, holding the initiative, Fighter Command could assemble its forces at times of its own choosing and direct them for maximum effect.

Above left: Bader's Spitfire, carrying his initials on the rear fuselage.

Left: Wing Commander Douglas Bader, third from the left, led the Tangmere Wing in the Target Support role during Circus 62. He is seen here a week before the operation with, from the left, Flying Officer 'Johnnie' Johnson and Flight Lieutenant 'Cocky' Dundas. The officer on the far right was Lieutenant Llewellyn, an observer from the US Army Air Force (at that time the USA was still neutral).

At 27,000 feet, high above the bombers and their immediate escorts, flew the Spitfires of the Biggin Hill Wing (Nos 72, 92 and 609 Squadrons). These, with the Spitfires of the Hornchurch Wing (Nos 403 (Canadian), 603 and 611 Squadrons) and the Tangmere Wing (Nos 41, 610 and 616 Squadrons), comprised the target support force whose task was to establish air superiority in the general area of the target during the attack. Whilst the Biggin Hill Wing was to move in with the bombers, the other two were to cross the French coast at Le Touquet and, sweeping eastwards high over the German airfields, engage the enemy fighters as they came up.

The three Target Support Wings, comprising more than a hundred Spitfires, were out looking for trouble. But the small German fighter force remaining in the west, outnumbered and with orders to conserve its resources, refused to be drawn into a pitched battle. Instead the fighter *Gruppen,* enjoying the assistance of ground radar, concentrated on harrying the raiders and picking off stragglers. The subsequent report from the Tangmere Wing, commanded during this operation by Wing Commander Douglas Bader, illustrates well the sort of spasmodic action which resulted:

Wing met over base, crossed the English coast over Hastings at 23/24/25000 feet and made a landfall over Le Touquet at 23/24/27000 feet. A large orbit was made between Merville and Le Touquet. Proceeded towards the target area, encountering many Me 109s approximately 1,000 feet above. Enemy aircraft came down out of the sun on the starboard quarter; the Wing turned to attack and the enemy aircraft dived away refusing to engage, but dogfights ensued. These tactics ensued over the Hazebrouck, Merville and Lille areas and on the way back to the French coast, where the 109s broke away. The coast was recrossed by squadrons separately between Le Touquet and Boulogne; all the pilots and aircraft had returned by 18.55, with the exception of one from 41 Squadron.

The Biggin Hill and Hornchurch Wings fought similarly inconclusive engagements.

In the mean time the Blenheims were able to reach Lille unmolested by enemy fighters, only to find their target shrouded in cloud. Without bombing

Above: Spitfire Mk Vs of No 603 Squadron which, operating as part of the Hornchurch Wing, took part in Circus 62.

Right: Squadron Leader Rankin (without jacket, left) with Flight Lieutenant Charles Kingcombe, lighting cigarettes immediately after their return to Biggin Hill from an operation over northern France in the summer of 1941. During Circus 62 Rankin was credited with the destruction of one Messerschmitt 109 and with causing damage to a second.

they withdrew north-westwards along the planned route and attacked their alternative target: invasion barges moored in the canal at Gravelines.

Positioned to cover the initial phase of the withdrawal were two Polish-manned Spitfire squadrons from Northolt (Nos 306 and 308), which made up the Forward Support Wing. While the Blenheims were closing on Gravelines No 308 Squadron was the object of a particularly sharp attack during which an estimated eighteen Messerschmitts 'bounced' the Spitfires and, in the brisk action which followed, shot down two before the Poles could retaliate.

Covering the final phase of the withdrawal was the Rear Support Wing, comprising one Spitfire and two Hurricane Squadrons (respectively Nos 19, 257 and 401 (Canadian)) drawn from No 12 Group. This wing also came under attack and lost two Spitfires and a Hurricane.

From start to finish, the incursion over German-held France had lasted just over half an hour. During that time a force of more than two hundred RAF aircraft had drawn into battle a considerably smaller number of German fighters, claiming to have destroyed three of them and probably destroyed three more; this, at a cost of six British aircraft destroyed and their pilots killed or captured.

Truely, Circus No 62 cannot be considered as one of the more impressive feats of British arms. Yet it would be unwise to judge the value of such operations as a simple profit-and-loss account. In war a fighting force must be given the opportunity to fight, or its spirit will wither and die; by keeping Fighter Command in action in this way, even if the terms were unfavourable, Sir Sholto Douglas ensured that his pilots remained combat-hardened during the difficult period following the Battle of Britain.

Above: During 1941 the Spitfire squadrons of Fighter Command gradually re-equipped with the Mark V and this version bore the brunt of the offensive operations over northern France that summer. This particular aircraft, serial R6923, was one of the original cannon-armed Mark Is which fought during the early part of the Battle of Britain with No 19 Squadron. After her withdrawal from operations she was modified to Mark V standard by the fitting of a more-powerful Merlin 45 engine and, with a modified feed system to the Hispano cannon, was re-issued to No 92 Squadron early the following year. At the controls when this photograph was taken was Squadron Leader Jimmy Rankin, the commander of No 92 Squadron.

Above: A Messerschmitt 109F pictured going down in flames before the guns of a Spitfire; during Circus 62 RAF pilots reported shooting down three aircraft of this type and damaging three others. The 'F' model of the famous German fighter was a slightly re-designed and more powerful version of the 'E' which had fought during the Battle of Britain and was comparable in performance with the Mark V Spitfire.

Above: This Spitfire IIB, which belonged to the Polish No 306 Squadron, made an emergency landing at Biggin Hill in August 1941. She had suffered five hits from 20mm rounds, two of them explosive, and numerous hits from machine gun bullets. Note the effect of the two explosive shells, on the rudder and the port tailplane. The latter had blown away almost the entire lower surface and must have made control in pitch very difficult. (Unfortunately more details of the cause of the damage could not be found, in spite of an intensive search, because apparently some Polish units did not consider such 'minor' battle damage worthy of mention in their diaries).

Top right: A Mark V Spitfire undergoing a 30-hour inspection, probably at Hornchurch early in 1942. The fitters and riggers can be seen working through their long lists of items requiring checking. For example, the engine cowlings have been removed for examination to allow the oil filter to be removed and cleaned, and the engine to be checked for possible oil, fuel or coolant leaks; the propeller spinner has been removed to allow checking for possible damage, or leakage from the hydraulic pitch-change mechanism.

Below: A few days, but greatly differing circumstances, separate these two photographs. An RAF ground crewman points out that the victory tally on the Wing Commander Stanford-Tuck's Spitfire stands at twenty-nine, but the total was never to get any higher. On January 28th 1942, just over a month after his final kill, Stanford-Tuck's engine was hit by ground fire during a strafing attack. As he was gliding in for a crash landing a Flak emplacement opened up on him so Stanford-Tuck kicked his nose round and gave the gunners a quick 'squirt' before he hit the ground; he later learned that a chance round had gone right down the slim barrel of the German 20mm gun and split it open.

German gunners, doubtless impressed by Stanford-Tuck's markmanship, examine the mount of their fallen adversary. As commander of the Biggin Hill Wing, Robert Stanford-Tuck carried his initials on his aircraft.

Below left: Squadron Leader P. Davies, who commanded No 19 Squadron during much of 1942, pictured in an early version of the 'K' Type dinghy issued to Spitfire pilots. On a smooth millpond like the one seen here, the greatest discomfort from riding in such a craft was likely to be a wet behind; in an open sea, without protection from the wind and spray, such a craft could be the lonliest and most dispiriting place on earth. Yet the necessity for the dinghy could not be argued: a Mae West lifejacket would prevent a man from drowning, but that was all it would do; if he wore normal flying kit his period of useful consciousness in the waters round Britain could be as little as two hours during the summer months, falling to about 45 minutes during the winter. Later versions of the 'K' Type dinghy carried a simple apron to provide the survivor with some protection from the elements. Probably the record for time adrift in a single-seat dinghy, as a survivor, is held by a Pole: Flight Lieutenant L. Kurylowicz of No 316 Squadron; he baled out of his Spitfire over mid-Channel in the autumn of 1943 and, following a gruelling battle for life during which he rode out a near-gale, was finally rescued after eighty-five hours in the water.

Left: Each morning the Spitfires had to be run up to high revs on the ground to check the operation of the propeller constant speed unit and the two magnetos, with two or more ground crewmen serving as 'breathing ballast' holding down the tail. Pleasant enough on a warm sunny day, this task could be a miserable one on a bitterly cold winter's morning.

Right: A reconnaissance Spitfire pictured in her element, high above the earth. If possible when over enemy territory, reconnaissance pilots preferred to fly just underneath the thin layer of sky where condensation trails form; in that way they could expect a little extra warning of the approach of enemy aircraft trying to 'bounce' them from above.

Spitfire Spyplane

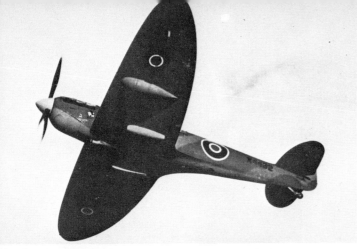

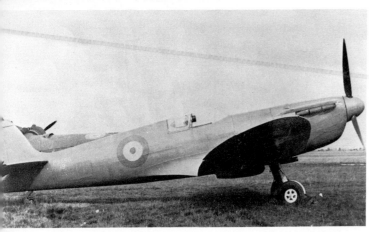

Above: These three Spitfires had originally been ordered as fighters, Mark Is; but prior to delivery were modified into the photographic reconnaissance Type C by the removal of all guns and armour and the installation of extra fuel tanks in and under the wings and two vertical cameras in the rear fuselage. Some aircraft were adapted to carry cameras in the underwing tanks. During 1941 all three Spitfires were further modified to PR Type F standard by the addition of a 29 gallon fuel tank under the pilot's seat, a deeper nose cowling to house the larger oil tank necessary for the longer flights, additional oxygen bottles and a new canopy with side blisters. All three were Type F Spitfires when these photographs were taken. Top: X4492, showing clearly her port underwing fuel tank. Centre: X4498, pictured at the time in July 1941 when she belonged to No 3 Photographic Reconnaissance Unit at Oakington, with Squadron Leader R. Elliott at the controls. Above: P9550, one of the very early PR Spitfire conversions, had begun operations with A Flight of the original Photographic Reconnaissance Unit in July 1940, flying from Wick in northern Scotland; now modified to Type F standard, her bulged nose for the extra oil tank is clearly shown.

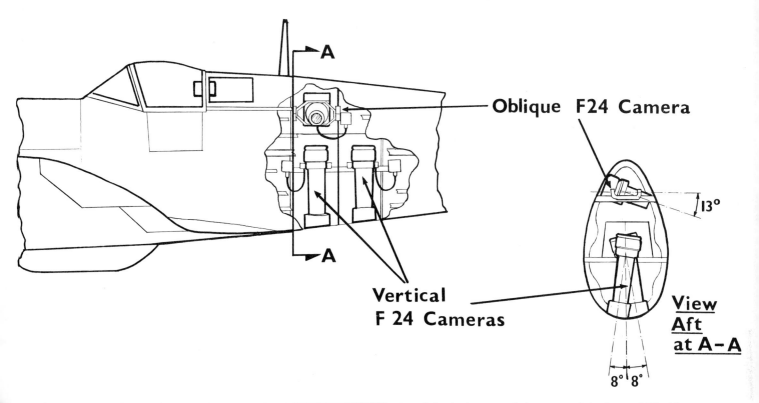

Oblique F24 Camera

Vertical F 24 Cameras

13°

View Aft at A-A

8° 8°

Top left: A close-up of the fuselage of a PR Type F, showing the access hatch for the vertically mounted cameras; note also the bulge on the side of the canopy, to enable the pilot to see directly underneath the aircraft for vertical photography.

Above: Spitfire camera mountings for photographic reconnaissance. Basically there were two types of mounting: vertical or oblique, the latter for low-altitude photography. The drawing here shows both types of camera mountings with one oblique and two vertical although; so far as is known, no Spitfire in service ever carried cameras for both oblique and vertical photography at the same time because access to the lower cameras for servicing would have been very awkward. The vertical cameras shown here were two F24s and this was known as the X fitting; if two smaller F8 cameras were installed this was known as the W fitting and the majority of PR Spitfires used for medium-high altitude reconnaissance had one of these two fitments.

Some of the classic reconnaissance photographs

of the Second World War were taken from Spitfires.

Centre left: Into the valley of the shadow of death . . . : a remarkably clear picture of the German heavy cruiser Hipper in dry dock, taken by Pilot Officer J. Chandler on January 26th 1941 as he flew low over the heavily defended port of Brest.

Far left Bottom: the famous photograph of the Wuerzburg radar set at the top of the cliffs at Bruneval, taken on December 5th 1941 by Flight Lieutenant Tony Hill, which led to a commando attack and its capture.

Left: a further 'scoop' by Hill: taken on May 2nd 1942 over the Dutch island of Walcheren, this picture was the first to reach Britain to show the details of the Giant Wuerzburg radar used to control Luftwaffe night fighters; the startled operator (bottom right) about to mount the steps later served as a human yardstick and made it possible for interpreters to measure the exact size of the reflector dish—and thus deduce the radar's operating characteristics.

Above: Men of a Luftwaffe salvage unit seen removing a Spitfire which had come down in northern France. This particular aircraft was shot down near St Omer in April 1942, during a fight with Fw 190s; the pilot, Flight Lieutenant Kustrzynski of the Polish No 303 Squadron, was taken prisoner.

Outclassed

War is no respector of reputations. If an opponent introduces greatly improved equipment, a position of air superiority can be translated into one of inferiority in a matter of weeks. That began to happen to RAF Fighter Command in the autumn of 1941, as the German fighter *Gruppen* in France gradually re-equipped with the Focke Wulf 190. In June 1942 the RAF secured an airworthy example of this new German fighter and within days of its capture it was undergoing hastily-arranged combat trials with each of the operational Allied fighters. Reproduced below is the report by the Air Fighting Development Unit on the trial of the Fw 190 against the Spitfire V, which illustrates in stark terms the measure of the inferiority of Fighter Command's equipment during most of the third year of the war.

The Fw 190 was compared with a Spitfire VB from an operational squadron for speed and all-round manoeuvrability at heights up to 25,000 feet. The Fw 190 is superior in speed at all heights, and the approximate differences are listed as follows:-

At 1,000 ft the Fw 190 is 25-30mph faster than the Spitfire VB.
At 3,000 ft the Fw 190 is 30-35mph faster than the Spitfire VB.
At 5,000 ft the Fw 190 is 25mph faster than the Spitfire VB.
At 9,000 ft the Fw 190 is 25-30mph faster than the Spitfire VB (second blower in operation).
At 15,000 ft the Fw 190 is 20mph faster than the Spitfire VB.
At 18,000 ft the Fw 190 is 20mph faster than the Spitfire VB.
At 21,000 ft the Fw 190 is 25mph faster than the Spitfire VB.
At 25,000 ft the Fw 190 is 20-25mph faster than the Spitfire VB.

Climb The climb of the Fw 190 is superior to that of the Spitfire VB at all heights. The best speeds for climbing

are approximately the same, but the angle of the Fw 190 is considerably steeper. Under maximum continuous climbing conditions the climb of the Fw 190 is about 450ft/min better up to 25,000 feet.

With both aircraft flying at high cruising speed and then pulling up into a climb, the superior climb of the Fw 190 is even more marked. When both aircraft are pulled up into a climb from a dive, the Fw 190 draws away very rapidly and the pilot of the Spitfire has no hope of catching it.

Dive Comparative dives between the two aircraft have shown that the Fw 190 can leave the Spitfire with ease, particularly during the initial stages.

Manoeuverability The manoeuverability of the Fw 190 is better than that of the Spitfire VB except in turning circles, If on the other hand the Spitfire was flying at maximum continuous cruising and was 'bounced' under the same conditions, it had a reasonable chance of avoiding being caught by opening the

throttle and going into a *shallow* dive, provided the Fw 190 was seen in time. This forced the Fw 190 into a stern chase and although it eventually caught the Spitfire, it took some time and as a result was drawn a considerable distance away from its base. This is a particularly useful method of evasion for the Spitfire if it is 'bounced' when returning from a sweep. This manoeuvre has been carried out during recent operations and has been successful on several occasions.

If the Spitfire VB is 'bounced' it is thought unwise to evade by diving steeply, as the Fw 190 will have little difficulty in catching up owing to its superiority in the dive.

The above trials have shown that the Spitfire VB must cruise at high speed when in an area where enemy fighters can be expected. It will then, in addition to lessening the chances of being successfully 'bounced', have a better chance of catching the Fw 190, particularly if it has the advantage of surprise.

Above: After Circus 101, flown on September 21st 1941, returning pilots of the Polish No 315 Squadron reported engaging an '. . . unknown enemy aircraft with a radial engine.' The RAF would soon learn to know and respect the Focke Wulf 190 which, it soon became clear, almost completely outclassed the Spitfire Mark V—the best aircraft Fighter Command then had operational.

To See Was to Live

Left: With so much at stake, the cleaning of the canopy assumed an almost ritualistic importance prior to an operational sortie. A fragile material, perspex could be scratched unwittingly even by wiping it with a handkerchief; only the very softest of cloths could be used for cleaning it.

Above right: This is why fighter pilots demanded that their canopies and windscreens be absolutely clean and brightly transparent. Hold this photograph 18 inches away from your face, out to one side. Now, imagine that you are in a Spitfire over enemy territory, liable to be 'bounced' at any time. You begin your systematic search of the sky, beginning at the left and the rear. Your eyes move in a slow and deliberate up-and-down zig-zag movement, sweeping from high above to below the horizon and working round clockwise until you get to the right and the rear; then you search once more in the direction of the sun, glance into the cockpit to check that all is still well there and begin all over again. Your life depends upon the efficiency of your search: if an enemy fighter ever reaches a position where its size is that shown in the photograph it will be 600 yards away, with its pilot just about to open fire; if he gets any closer without your seeing him, the chances are that your epitaph will be a simple victory bar painted on his aircraft when he gets home. Whatever the romantics might have one believe, air fighting is a rough and nasty business with no quarter given; the 'sitting duck' usually ended up as a 'dead duck'.

Although the side perspex might appear transparent when looking at objects down sun, Top right, a glance at the same objects into sun soon revealed the extent of light-scattering due to even the slightest scratching on the hood.

A problem, and a solution. Oil slinging was a common occurance from the constant-speed propellers fitted to Spitfires. In the photograph (Below) taken immediately after a fight, the left half of the windscreen had been cleaned while the right half had had the oil left on; note the deterioration in visibility caused by the oil. Some Spitfires, like this one (Below right) were fitted with a simple locally-made oil collector ring to prevent the oil from spraying on the windscreen.

Production Testing

Alex Henshaw, MBE

A brand-new Mark V pictured immediately after take-off from Castle Bromwich.

Those fortunate enough to have watched Alex Henshaw display a Spitfire still talk about the experience, for he is acknowledged to be a virtuoso in the art of aerobatics. During his six-year career as a production and development test pilot he came to know the Spitfire as few men can have done — which is hardly surprising, considering the fact that he personnally test flew more than one in ten of all of those built.

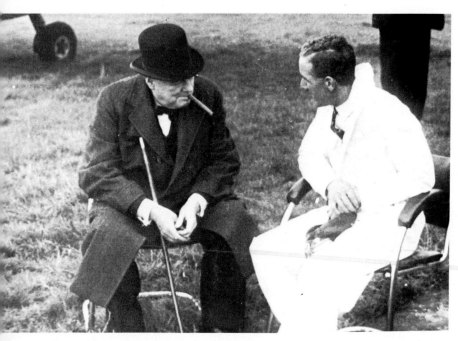

Above: Alex Henshaw discussing his work with Mr Churchill, when the latter paid a visit to the Castle Bromwich plant.

I learned to fly at my own expense at the age of twenty, and during the years that followed flying occupied most of my spare time. During the 1930s a skilful and resourceful pilot with money or suitable sponsors could make a name for himself in aviation. I became very enthusiastic about competition flying and enjoyed a run of successes culminating in the winning of the King's Cup in 1938. In the following year I took the records for the flight from London to Cape Town and return; for the solo flight, these records still stand in 1973.

When the war came I accepted a job with Vickers as a test pilot and after testing Wellingtons at Weybridge and Spitfires and Walruses at Southampton, in the summer of 1940 I became Chief Test Pilot at the new Spitfire factory at Castle Bromwich. During the years that

followed I became responsible, in addition, for flight testing the Spitfires built at Cosford and Desford, the Seafires at South Marsden and the repaired aircraft at Cowley. I remained at this work until 1946, by which time I had flown a total of 2,360 different Spitfires and Seafires — more than one in ten of all of those built.

As a production test pilot, one's task is really that of flight inspector; one has to satisfy oneself that everything works as it should and that the aircraft behaves as it was designed to. Unless there was some unforeseen snag, the flight test procedure for the Spitfire was straight-forward. The procedure differed somewhat from mark to mark, so in this description I shall confine myself to that for the Mark V.

After a thorough pre-flight check I would take off and, once at circuit height, I would trim the aircraft and try to get her to fly straight-and-level with hands off the stick. The Mark V lacked aileron trim tabs and most of the new ones had a tendency to fly with one wing low. When that happened I would land immediately and taxi to one corner of the airfield, where a mechanic would be waiting. He carried a special tool rather like a tuning fork, and on my instruction he would bend the trailing edge of the

aileron on his side once, twice or thrice, up or down. Then he would go round to the other side, and similarly bend the opposite aileron in the other direction. That done I would take off again and trim the aircraft to fly hands-off, to see whether the wing dropping had been cleared; usually it had, but if it had not the process was repeated until the trim was acceptable (sometimes, if bending alone was not sufficient, it was necessary to change the ailerons). It was a Heath Robinson system, but it did work.

Once the trim was satisfactory, I would take the Spitfire up in a full throttle climb at 2,850rpm to the rated altitude of the one or both supercharger blowers. Then I would make a careful check of the power output from the engine, calibrated for height and temperature. Many factors could give a false reading: a leaking boost gauge line, a high ambient temperature, a faultily calibrated rev-counter, or even an incorrectly set-up altimeter. If all appeared satisfactory, I would then put her into a dive at full power and 3,000rpm, and trim her to fly hands and feet off at 460 mph IAS. Unless this was all right, adjustments would be necessary to the elevator trim; or slight dressing down might be needed to the trailing edge of the tailplane.

Personally, I never cleared a Spitfire unless I had carried out a few aerobatic tests to determine how good or how bad she was; but the extent of this depended upon how tired or how rushed we were.

The production test was usually quite a brisk affair: the initial circuit lasted less than ten minutes and the main flight took between twenty and thirty minutes. Then the aircraft received a final once-over by our ground mechanics, any faults were rectified, and the Spitfire was ready for collection. Sometimes I would make more than twenty such test flights in a single day, necessary if previous bad weather had stopped flying and, with the production line going at full blast, the number of aircraft awaiting testing begain to mount.

As I have said, unless there was some unforeseen snag the flight test procedure was usually straightforward. But we did get the odd problem that gave us a lot of worry before we could get it sorted out. For example, there was one Spitfire which had been returned to us with a report that she behaved all right at normal speeds, but in high-speed dives she vibrated to such an extent that it seemed about to break up; a complete wing-change had been suggested. We at Castle Bromwich treated the report with some reserve; besides, a wing-change

During the Second World War men and women were drafted into the aircraft factories from all walks of life and, considering the sketchy training many of them received, the quality of the end product was remarkably high. These standards were the result of extreme specialisation by members of the work force, jigging for even the simplest of tasks, and rigorous inspection.

Below left: women putting together the port wing of a Spitfire.

Below: Seamstresses in the fabric shop, covering rudders.

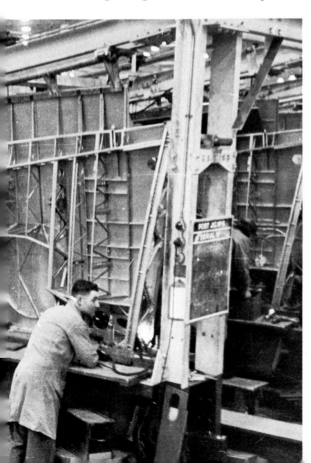

Above: Test pilots walking
out to the aircraft, at the
start of a day's flying at
Castle Bromwich; Alex
Henshaw is second from the
right. The Spitfire in the
background was to have a
nomadic career: delivered
to the RAF in May 1942
she went to No 66 Squadron
in August, No 312 Squadron
in October and No 167
Squadron in November; the
following year she served
with Nos 132 and 146
Squadrons and, in 1944, she
flew with Nos 501 and 345
Squadrons before being sent
to No 61 Operational
Training Unit. She was
scrapped in July 1945.

was a major job and we wanted to be sure
that the fault could not be cleared by less
drastic measures. However, when two of
my experienced test pilots confirmed the
seriousness of the vibration (one had even
prepared to bail out), I knew we had to
take the report seriously. I took the
Spitfire up and, as everyone had said, at
normal speeds every dial and gauge read
correctly and her performance was
average for the mark. I did some mild
aerobatics and still everything seemed to
be normal. So I stepped up the
aerobatics, and as I dived preparatory to
some vertical rolls there was a sudden
bang like an explosion; there was a
terrible row and the Spitfire seemed to
vibrate so violently that I hastily
prepared to bail out. I pulled out of the
dive and then, as suddenly as it had
began, the staccato noise and vibration
ceased. It was all very mysterious. I flew

around for a while mulling over the
matter, and finally decided to do a series
of dives from high level and take down
some figures; so far as I was able, I
prepared myself for a possible break-up.
At about 430mph in the first such dive
the vibration set in again and I had to
brace myself against the cockpit to take
the figures I wanted. As I did so I found
that I could read all the gauges quite
easily; the readings were all normal.
Gradually it dawned on me that while
there was some vibration, the worst part
of the problem was the staccato sound;
and while the latter was certainly
disturbing to the pilot, it appeared to be
quite unharmful to the machine.
Momentarily I took my hands off the
controls and pressed them over the ear
pads of my flying helmet to damp out the
sound; to my surprise and intense relief,
the Spitfire seemed to be behaving like

speed built up it would flap vigorously between the armour plating and the nearly empty fuel tank; and if that happened it would almost certainly give rise to the sort of kettle-drumming noise we had experienced. I immediately landed and had the tank top-cover removed; sure enough, the self-sealer had come adrift. With a new fuel tank fitted, she proved to be a perfectly ordinary Spitfire.

I loved the Spitfire, in every one of her many versions. But it has to be admitted that the later marks did not handle quite so nicely as the earlier ones had done. One test of manoeuverability was to throw her into a flick roll, and see how many times she rolled. With a Mark II or a Mark V one got two and a half flick rolls, but the later Mark IX was heavier and you got only one and a half; with the later and still heavier marks one got even less. Similarly with the earlier versions one could take off and go straight into a half loop and roll off the top, but the later Spitfires were much too heavy for that. The essence of aircraft design is compromise and an improvement at one end of the performance envelope is rarely obtained without a deterioration somewhere else.

any other at that speed. I felt that I now had the key to the problem. But where was the noise coming from? I climbed the Spitfire again and took her into a third dive, and this time I felt all round the cockpit and thought I could feel a hard persistent hammering near the engine. I was however sure that the banging had nothing to do with the engine or the airscrew, for these had been changed earlier without curing the problem. It seemed to be coming from the engine bulkhead — or perhaps the main petrol tank. Then it came to me with such simplicity and suddenness that I couldn't resist shouting at myself for being such a bloody fool and not guessing the reason earlier. The top of the upper petrol tank had a thick outer covering of hard rubber self-sealer, and above it was a heavy piece of bullet-proof plating. If the self-sealer had become partially detatched, as the

Below: Spitfire EP 615 did not reach the RAF! On August 18th 1942, during a transit flight between Cosford and Castle Bromwich, Alex Henshaw suffered an engine failure. He tried to belly land between some houses near Willenhall but unfortunately an open camera flap caused one wing to stall first and drop, as he was committed to his final approach. The Spitfire struck a large tree which tore off the starboard wing, smashed into a nearby house, careered through the kitchen garden shedding pieces as she did so and finally came to rest in a field. Remarkably, in view of the damage to the aircraft, Henshaw escaped with only cuts, bruises and a severe shaking.

The Balance Restored

Right: On August 19th 1942 Allied forces launched a large scale 'reconnaissance in force' on the French port of Dieppe, under a defensive umbrella provided by RAF Fighter Command. A total of forty-eight squadrons of Spitfires took part in the operation: forty-two with the Mark V, two with the Mark VI and four with the Mark IX. Throughout the day the fighters warded off repeated German attempts to attack the mass of shipping off the coast. In the photograph (top right) a Dornier 217 is seen under attack by a Spitfire; (bottom right), the same aircraft going down with its port engine belching smoke.

Below: Mark IX Spitfires of No 611 Squadron, one of the first units to receive the type.

The supremacy of the Focke Wulf 190 over the Spitfires lasted from September 1941 until July 1942, when No 64 Squadron received the first of the Mark IX Spitfires to enter service. With an airframe similar to that of the Mark V, the Mark IX was fitted with the new Merlin 61 engine which employed a two-stage supercharger using two centrifugal impellors in series. The new engine gave a substantial improvement in high altitude performance over the Merlin 46, which powered the Spitfire Mark V: at 30,000 feet the Merlin 46 developed 720 horse power whereas the Merlin 61 developed 1,020 — an improvement of more than forty per cent. This extra power was sufficient to close the gap in performance between the Spitfires and the Fw 190. Indeed, as this Air Fighting Development Unit report shows, the performance of these two fighters were now about as close as they could possibly be, considering the fact that they were quite different aircraft.

The Fw 190 was compared with a full operational Spitfire IX for speed and manoeuverability at heights up to 25,000 feet. The Spitfire IX at most heights is slightly superior in speed to the Fw 190 and the approximate differences in speeds at various heights are as follows: -

At 2,000ft the Fw 190 is 7-8mph faster than the Spitfire IX.
At 5,000ft the Fw 190 and the Spitfire IX are approximately the same
At 8,000ft the Spitfire IX is 8mph faster than the Fw 190.
At 15,000ft the Spitfire IX is 5mph faster than the Fw 190.
At 18,000ft the Fw 190 is 3mph faster than the Spitfire IX.
At 21,000ft the Fw 190 and the Spitfire IX are approximately the same.
At 25,000ft the Spitfire IX is 5-7mph faster than the Fw 190.

Climb During comparative climbs at various heights up to 23,000 feet, with both aircraft flying under maximum continuous climbing conditions, little difference was found between the two aircraft although on the whole the Spitfire IX was slightly better. Above 22,000 feet the climb of the Fw 190 is

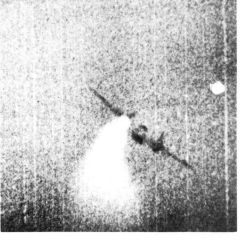

Below: As a measure to improve the performance of the Spitfire Mark V vis-a-vis the Fw 190, the wings of the former were 'clipped' by more than four feet. The modification increased the the rate of roll slightly, by reducing the inertia moment of the wing; it also increased the maximum speed by about 5mph up to 15,000 feet, though at the expense of both speed and rate of climb above 20,000 feet. Fitted with Merlins modified to give maximum power at low altitude, the clipped-winged version went into service designated the LF Mark V. She was not popular with those who flew her, however, and was referred to as the 'clipped, cropped and clapped Spitty'—referring to her shortened wings, the reduced size of the Merlin's supercharger blades and the fact that many of the aircraft had given their best during earlier service. This example belonged to No 315 (Polish) Squadron.

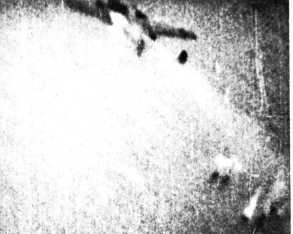

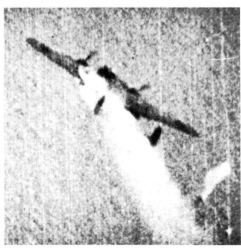

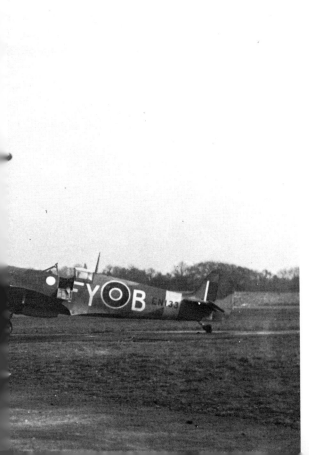

Below, right: High Endeavour. In 1940 the Luftwaffe took delivery of a small number of Junkers 86P high level reconnaissance aircraft and these began operations over the British Isles. Powered by two double supercharged two-stroke diesel engines, the Ju 86P could cruise at 36,000 feet; the later Ju 86R could cruise at 45,000 feet. The two-man crew was housed in a fully-pressurised cabin. These high-flying intruders and the ever-present possibility that the Germans might employ very-high-flying bombers in quantity, spurred the development of versions of the Spitfire for high altitude interception work. The Mark VI was the first specially-built variant of the Spitfire for high-altitude fighting and went into service in the spring of 1942. As well as a highly-supercharged version of the Merlin, the Mark VI was fitted with a pressure cabin and a longer-span wing; the latter was pointed, to reduce the strength (and therefore the drag) of the wing-tip vortices induced when flying at high angles of attack at high altitude. This example belonged to No 124 Squadron, one of the few units to receive the version.

Left: Squadron Leader Herbert Hallowes commanded No 222 Squadron during the Dieppe action and was credited with one Do 217 shot down and a further one damaged. He ended the war holding the rank of Wing Commander, credited with twenty-one victories.

falling off rapidly, whereas the climb of the Spitfire IX is increasing. When both aircraft were flying at high cruising speed and were pulled up into a climb from level flight, the Fw 190 had a slight advantage in the initial stages of the climb due to its better acceleration. This superiority was slightly increased when both aircraft were pulled up into the climb from a dive.

It must be appreciated that the differences between the two aircraft are only slight and that in actual combat the advantage in climb will be with the aircraft that has the initiative.

Dive The Fw 190 is faster than the Spitfire IX in a dive, particularly during the initial stage. This superiority is not as marked as with the Spitfire VB.

Manoeuverability The Fw 190 is more manoeuverable than the Spitfire IX except in turning circles, when it is out-turned without difficulty.

The superior rate of roll of the Fw 190 enabled it to avoid the Spitfire IX if attacked when in a turn, by flicking over into a diving turn in the opposite direction and, as with the Spitfire VB, the Spitfire IX had great difficulty in following this manoeuvre. It would have been easier for the Spitfire IX to follow the Fw 190 in the diving turn if its engine had been fitted with a negative 'G' carburettor, as this type of engine

with the ordinary carburettor cuts very easily.

The Spitfire IX's worst heights for fighting the Fw 190 were between 18,000 and 22,000 feet and below 3,000 feet. At these heights the Fw 190 is a little faster.

Both aircraft 'Bounced' one another in order to ascertain the best avasive tactics to adopt. The Spitfire IX could not be caught when 'bounced' if it was cruising at high speed and saw the Fw 190 when well out of range. When the Spitfire IX was cruising at low speed its inferiority in acceleration gave the Fw 190 a reasonable chance of catching it up and the same applied if the position was reversed and the Fw 190 was 'bounced' by the Spitfire IX, except that the overtaking took a little longer.

The initial acceleration of the Fw 190 is better than the Spitfire IX under all conditions of flight, except that in level flight at such altitudes where the Spitfire has a speed advantage and then, provided the Spitfire is cruising at high speed, there is little to choose between the acceleration of the two aircraft.

The general impression gained by the pilots taking part in the trials is that the Spitfire IX compares favourably with the Fw 190 and that provided the Spitfire has the initiative, it undoubtedly has a good chance of shooting down the Fw 190.

Below: Malta Spitfires. The first fighter (as distinct from reconnaissance) Spitfires to deploy for operations overseas were those flown off the deck of the aircraft carrier HMS Eagle to Malta in March 1942. During that operation and in the months that followed a total of 275 Spitfires were delivered to the beleaguered island, by by Eagle and the USS Wasp; these were sufficient to break the back of the German air attack on Malta. When this photograph of No 126 Squadron's aircraft was taken, at Luqa in the late summer, Spitfires at readiness could even be lined up in the open without undue risk.

Eagle Squadron, Eighth Air Force

Ervin Miller

Left: This Spitfire of No 121 'Eagle' Squadron was photographed in September 1942, a few days before the unit was handed over to the USAAF where it became No 335 Fighter Squadron.

About a thousand Spitfires of various Marks saw service in the US Army Air Force during the Second World War. An American citizen, Ervin Miller flew Spitfires with No 133 'Eagle' Squadron of the Royal Air Force, remained with the unit when it was transferred to the US Eighth Air Force and became the 336th Fighter Squadron in September 1942 and saw the Squadron's Spitfires replaced by Thunderbolts in the spring of the following year. In this section he recounts one American's very personnal memories of the most famous British fighter.

A citizen of the then-neutral USA, I volunteered for service as a pilot in the Royal Air Force in 1940. I was a young man who had fallen head-over-heels in love with flying and my job at the time, that of a US Government equipment inspector, served merely as a means of getting money to pay for my time airborne. By the middle of 1940 I had amassed about four hundred flying hours in light aircraft. In volunteering for the

RAF I must admit I had no noble motives like helping defeat Nazism, or defending freedom, or anything like that. All I wanted to do was get my hands on a really high-performance aircraft (at that time entry as a pilot into the US Army Air Corps was very restricted; if one did not have a degree — and I did not — it was almost impossible).

Initially things moved very slowly and it was mid-1941 before I began my advanced flying course (paid for by the British government) at a private flying school at Tulsa, Oklahoma. Towards the end of the year I received the King's Commision as a Pilot Officer in the RAF and came to Britain for further training which culminated at the Spitfire Operational Training Unit at Llandow in the spring of 1942.

The following May I joined No 133 'Eagle' Squadron at Biggin Hill, which was operating Spitfire Vs; the commander, Squadron Leader 'Tommy' Thomas, and the ground crewmen were British, the rest of the pilots were American. After a period of familiaris-

Below: Second Lieutenant Ervin Miller, pictured at Debden in 1942 soon after his transfer to the USAAF from the RAF.

ation I began flying on operations in June, but not until the end of July did I see (or rather, take part in) an air combat. On the 28th we were operating as one of the support wings for a sweep over France when Focke Wulfs and Messerschmitts 'bounced' us. I was flying as No 2 to Flight Lieutenant Don Blakeslee, my Flight Commander*, and before take-off he had said to me "If we get bounced, for Christ's sake don't lose me." Well, we were 'bounced' — and I didn't lose him. I just hung on like a leech and all I recall of my first dogfight was the sight of his tailwheel; I don't think I even noticed a Jerry!

I flew on a few more operations then, in August, the Squadron received some exciting news: we were to re-equip with the new Mark IX Spitfire. I made my first flight in one on the 26th; she was a beauty. While the old Mark V became 'mushy' above 20,000 feet as the engine power began to fall away, the Mark IX

*Blakeslee later rose to the rank of Colonel in the USAF, and ended the war credited with fifteen victories in aerial combat.

with her more-powerful Merlin and two-stage supercharger just seemed to go on and on up. Conversion presented no problems; as soon as we had sufficient Mark IXs we were declared operational on type.

In the mean time, even more fundamental changes were in the wind. It had been decided at high level that the three RAF 'Eagle' Squadrons, Nos 71, 121 and 133, were to transfer to the US Army Air Force where they would become respectively the 334th, 335th and 336th Squadrons of the 4th Fighter Group to be based at Debden. A few of the pilots elected to stay in the RAF but the rest, myself included, made the switch.

Just before the hand-over ceremony, however, disaster struck No 133 Squadron. On September 26th we were ordered to send twelve Spitfires, plus two spares, to the airfield at Bolt Head in Devonshire; the latter was to serve as forward operating base for a routine covering patrol for Fortresses attacking a German airfield near Brest. Only twelve

Below: The first USAAF fighter unit to see action in Europe, as distinct from the American-manned but RAF controlled 'Eagle' Squadrons, was the 31st Fighter Group which became operational in August 1942. In this photo photograph two Spitfire Vs of No 307 Squadron, part of the Group, are seen about to take off from Manston for a sweep over France shortly after the unit became operational.

of the Spitfires were required for the operation and as I was about to walk out with the others my Flight Commander, Flight Lieutenant Marion Jackson, called over "You stay behind this time, Dusty." The drop-out from the other Flight, Don Gentile*, and I had both been itching to have a go at the Focke Wulfs with our new Spitfires and we begged not be be left behind. But the Flight Commanders were adamant: we would stay at Bolt Head. Don and I did not realise it, but our respective guardian angels were watching over us that day.

The Squadron started up and took off, then formed up and disappeared into the layer of cloud. On the ground Don and I kicked our heels until their planned time of return, but there was no sign of them. Then the Spitfire Vs of a Canadian Squadron engaged in the same operation

*Don Gentile ended the war as a Major, credited with twenty-one victories in air combat.

Below: Second Lieutenant Don Gentile, pictured shortly after his transfer from the RAF to the USAAF, with his Spitfire 'Buckeye-Don'. Gentile ended the war credited with twenty-one victories in air combat, making him the top scorer of the ex-'Eagle' Squadron pilots.

returned, late, on the very last of their fuel. When our Squadron's Spitfires' limit of endurance time came and went, with still no sign of them, we knew that something dreadful had happened. Then we heard that one of our pilots, Bob Beaty, had crash landed a few miles up the coast; he had run out of fuel, but managed to glide back the last few miles and had reached land.

Later we were able to piece together the story of what had happened to the others. The Squadron had set out over 10/10th cloud cover which concealed the ground features and, unknown to them, at their altitude there was a north-easterly jet-stream with winds of over 100mph. The Spitfires were blown far into the Bay of Biscay before, on ETA and having sighted nothing the leader, Flight Lieutenant Dick Brettell, turned round for home. He called one of the ground direction-finding stations for a steer and the one he received placed him about where he expected to be (a single direction-finder could not, of course, provide range). Again on ETA the formation closed-up and let down through the layer of cloud. When they emerged out the bottom they found themselves over land, which they took to

Above: A clipped-wing
Spitfire V of the 336th Fighter
Squadron, seen at Debden
following a landing accident
which collapsed the port
undercarriage leg.

be Cornwall. After a fruitless search for
their airfield the eleven Spitfires found a
large town, which they flew over at low
level in an attempt to get a fix; by that
time the aircraft were getting low on fuel.
Suddenly all Hell broke loose: the town
was the port of Brest, one of the most
heavily defended German positions in
France. Several of the Spitfires were shot
down immediately by *Flak* or fighters;
my good friend Gene Neville, who was
occupying my usual position as No 2 to
the Flight Commander, suffered a direct
hit from *Flak* and was killed instantly.
And those Spitfires which were not shot
down simply ran out of fuel and crashed.
Beaty had managed to get back only
because his engine was running roughly
and he had left the formation to return
early. For him, Don Gentile and me, it
had been a very narrow escape.

Following this incident the Spitfire IX,
with which Fighter Command had hoped
to take the Germans by surprise, came off
the secret list. Afterwards there was a full
court of inquiry. I understand that the
existence of the strong tail wind had been
known, but this vital information had
not been passed to the fighter squadrons.
I heard later that as a result some of the
Sector controllers received hasty postings

to insalubrious destinations in the Far
East.

The formal ceremony to hand the
'Eagle' Squadrons over to the USAAF
took place at Debden on September
29th, three days after the Brest disaster,
and it was a sadly depleted No 133
Squadron which took part. Moreover we
had had to leave our shiny new Mark IX
Spitfires at Biggin Hill and at Debden
there were only the old Mark Vs. We
were soon brought up to strength again
with replacement pilots, however, and
operations continued much as before.

From time to time we provided
support for the daylight bomber attacks
into occupied Europe; but the Spitfire
was so restricted in range that we could
not go where the action was. Of course
the Germans knew this and again and
again we saw them closing in on the
bombers as shortage of fuel forced us to
turn back.

One day in January 1943 General
Hunter, the Commander of the VIIIth
Fighter Command, came to visit us at
Debden. He said he had a 'surprise' for us
— we were soon to re-equip with the very
latest American fighter, the P-47
Thunderbolt. As he spoke we heard an
unusual engine note outside and one of

Spitfire Vs of the US 67th Tactical Reconnaissance Group which was based at Membury near Swindon from the autumn of 1942 until November 1943, as part of the Eighth Air Force. From time to time the unit's Spitfires took part in RAF fighter sweeps over northern France, though never in Group or Squadron strength.

the new fighters landed and taxied up beside one of our Spitfires. We went outside to look it over. It was huge: the wing tip of the P-47 came higher than the cockpit of the Spitfire. When we strapped into a Spitfire we felt snug and part of the aircraft; the Thunderbolt cockpit, on the other hand, was so large that we felt if we slipped off the Goddamned seat we would break a leg! We were horrified at the thought of going to war in such a machine: we had had enough trouble with the Focke Wulfs in our nimble Spitfire Vs; now this lumbering seven-ton monster seemed infinitely worse, a true 'air inferiority fighter'. Initial mock dog-fights between Thunderbolts and Spitfires seemed to confirm these feelings; we lost four Thunderbolt pilots in rapid succession, spinning in from low level while trying to match Spitfires in turns. In the end our headquarters issued an order banning mock dogfighting in Thunderbolts below 8,000 feet.

Gradually, however, we learnt how to fight in the Thunderbolt. At high altitude she was a 'hot ship' and very fast in the dive; the technique was not to 'mix it' with the enemy but to pounce on him from above, make one quick pass and get back up to altitude; if anyone tried to escape from a Thunderbolt by diving, we had him cold. Even more important, at last we had a fighter with the range to penetrate deeply into enemy territory — where the action was. So, reluctantly, we had to give up our beautiful little Spitfires and convert to the new juggernauts. The war was moving on and we had to move with it.

The change to the Thunderbolt might have been necessary militarily, but my heart remained with the Spitfire. Even now, thirty years after I flew them on operations, the mere sound or sight of a Spitfire brings me a deep feeling of nostalgia and many pleasant memories. She was such a gentle little aeroplane, without a trace of viciousness. She was a dream to handle in the air. I feel genuinely sorry for the modern fighter pilot who has never had the chance to get his hands on a Spitfire; he will never know what real flying was like.

Mediterranean Spits

Above: A Mark V, probably belonging to No 242 Group, pictured in Tunisia early in 1943. The aircraft was standing on the then-new Somerfield track used for the rapid construction of all-weather airfields; first the runway was rolled flat and covered with coir matting, then the operating surface of wire netting was laid on top.

Above right: Amongst the fighter units which went into Algeria and Morocco in November 1942 with the Allied invasion forces were two USAAF fighter Groups, the 31st and the 52nd equipped with the Spitfire V. This example belonged to the 308th Fighter Squadron, part of the 31st Fighter Group.

Right: This Spitfire, pictured undergoing an engine run at an RAF maintenance unit in North Africa, has the fuselage marking of the 52nd Fighter Group. However the wings carry RAF roundels, indicating that parts of more than one aircraft had been used to assemble this complete one.

Left: It was not easy to make a Spitfire look ugly. But Lieutenant R. Anderson of the US 52nd Fighter Group seems to have managed it with this hideous paint scheme for his Spitfire V.

Bottom left, Below: No 145 Squadron had been the first unit in North Africa to become operational with Spitfires, in June 1942. It was also the first to transfer to Sicily and these photographs show its Spitfires at the newly-prepared airfield at Pachino on July 13th 1943, just three days after the invasion of the island. Spitfires were operating from the airstrip even before the army engineers had finished rolling out the taxi ways.

After the 'Junkers Party'. On the morning of July 25th 1943 Wing Commander Colin Gray was leading a sweep by thirty-three Spitfires of No 322 Wing over north-eastern Sicily, when he stumbled upon a large force of Junkers 52 transports about to land at Milazzo. During the ensuing 'party', twenty-one of the transports and four escorts were shot down. Gray (centre), who accounted for two of the Ju 52s, is pictured with other pilots from his Wing who were successful that day.

Seen wearing what passed for uniform during the Italian campaign are the senior officers of the Spitfire-equipped No 244 Wing. From left to right: Squadron Leader 'Stan' Turner, commanding No 417 Squadron RCAF; Squadron Leader 'Hunk' Humphreys, No 92 Squadron; Wing Commander Wilfred Duncan-Smith, the Wing Leader; Group Captain Charles Kingcombe, commanding officer of the Wing; Squadron Leader Lance Wade, an American who commanded No 145 Squadron; and Major 'Bennie' Osler, a South African who commanded No 601 Squadron.

Ordeal by mud. Ground-crewmen of No 92 Squadron endeavouring to shift a Mark VIII which had become bogged down, probably at Canne in central Italy.

Spitfires of No 43 Squadron, pictured at Capodichino near Naples during the winter of 1943; in the background is Mount Vesuvius.

Left: A Spitfire V of a USAAF unit in Italy, with General Doolittle at the controls; the General had asked to 'try his hand' at flying the nimble little fighter.

Right: A Mark IX Spitfire operated by the 309th Squadron of the 31st Fighter Group in Italy.

Below: Four-cannon Spitfire Vs of No 2 Squadron, South African Air Force, pictured in line-astern formation over the Adriatic.

Centre right: After the invasion of Italy in 1943 many Spitfires were used for ground attack work and, as was common in the area, local modifications were often made. Shown here is a Spitfire V of 126 squadron modified by the unit personnel to carry a 250lb bomb under each wing. On the one shown here, the arming wire attached to the front of the bomb prevented the small nose vane from turning which, after a certain number of revolutions, would set the fuse to "live". When the bomb was dropped normally, the wire remained with the aircraft; but if the pilot had to jettison his bombs over friendly territotry he was able to select a "safe" setting which caused an electrical solenoid to release the arming wire from the aircraft. This prevented the vane from turning after the bomb left the aircraft to ensure that no big bang ensued! This particular bomb was subsequently dropped "live" on a radar station in Albania.

Below left: The makeshift arrangements for field maintenance are well illustrated here. Again, this is 126 squadron at Grottaglie in March 1944. There are many interesting points to note in the photograph: the battered oil-drum holding up the rear fuselage, and the two serviceable radiator units about to be fitted—an awkward job. Behind the ladder is the pilot's seat mounting; on the starboard wing is the long handle for the hydraulic hand-pump used for retraction tests, and also a cannon feed-drum for the starboard gun which has been removed. One of the most useful tools—a tommy-bar—is lying on the right-hand edge of the workbench and it is simply an old .303 Browning machine-gun barrel.

Below: Showing off her pointed wing-tips, this HF Mark VIII of No 417 Squadron RCAF is seen retracting her undercarriage immediately after take off from her base in Italy.

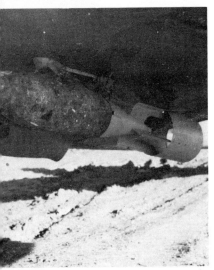

Defending Down Under

Left: Early in 1943 No 54 Squadron arrived in Darwin, Northern Australia, to take part in the defence of the area against Japanese attacks. In this photograph, one of the Squadron's Mark Vs is pictured just outside her camouflaged dispersal.

Bottom left: Early in 1944 No 54 Squadron re-equipped with Spitfire VIIIs. This interesting photograph, probably taken at Darwin, shows one of these aircraft with a four-cannon armament and pointed wing-tips for high altitude work.

Far left: Flight Lieutenant Tony Foster, left, was one of the more successful pilots of No 54 Squadron; credited with 3½ aircraft destroyed during the Battle of Britain, he opened the unit's score in the Far East on February 6th when he shot down a high-flying Japanese reconnaissance aircraft. He is seen here chatting to Flying Officer Tony Hughes.

Right: The overhead camouflage netting throws an interesting pattern of shadows on this Spitfire being readied at her dispersal at Darwin.

Left: The Spitfire flown by the commander of No 54 Squadron, Squadron Leader Eric Gibbs, being pushed into her dispersal.

Below: Taxiying out for take-off.

An Aerodynamicist's View

Sir Morien Morgan, CB MA CEng FRAeS

From the time of her first flight, to well after the end of the Second World War, the Spitfire was continually modified to improve her fighting ability. In this section Sir Morien Morgan summarises these changes, and throws a new light on the basic reason for the Spitfire's long and successful service career.

In 1935 I joined the Aerodynamics Flight at the Royal Aircraft Establishment at Farnborough and from the start specialised in aircraft stability and handling. At that time there were several new monoplanes being built — including the Spitfire — which flew faster, climbed faster, and landed much faster than the biplanes that preceded them. I remember that there was a terrific rush to develop these new aeroplanes and learn their foibles, to telescope the whole business of background research, design, pilot training and the rest of it; looking back, I am amazed that everyone did as well as they did — the designers, the research people and, of course, the pilots.

Let me give an example of the sort of mistaken ideas that got around early in the life of the Spitfire. We at Farnborough worked closely with the Aeroplane and Armament Experimental Establishment at Martlesham Heath, where they did the preliminary trials on the Spitfire and the other new military aircraft. I remember being there one day and talking to a very experienced RAF aerobatic pilot who had been involved with the tied-together formation aerobatic displays at Hendon. He had just landed after his first flight in the Spitfire prototype, utterly convinced that the days of close formation flying in fighters were numbered; he had handled his throttle in the same way as he did in a biplane and the much cleaner Spitfire had taken so long to lose speed that he thought close formation flying in such an aeroplane would be impossible. I was a young man at the time and what he said made a great impression on me: what effect would *this* have on future aerial combat? Later, when Martlesham had two or three Spitfires, they tried flying them in formation; and there was no real problem. I think the lesson here is that it is important for the pilots to get their hands on a new aircraft; when they do, it is surprising how fast they are able to adapt themselves to new conditions.

Looking back, I think that the greatest problem at the end of the 1930s was that it was extremely difficult to visualise what combat would be like in the new monoplane fighters; the only air fighting experts we had were from the First World War and that had been twenty years earlier. I think we all paid to much attention to the behaviour of an aeroplane flying on a calm sunny day and

harmonising the controls so that they could do nice aerobatic displays; we seemed to miss the importance of handling at speeds around the maximum permissable, in fast dives. Before the war, I remember, people thought that it was rather an academic exercise to scream downhill at one's maximum permissable speed.

The war soon brought us face to face with reality: once our fighter pilots started to mix it with the enemy they found that their main adversary, the Messerschmitt 109 which was less manoeuverable than the Spitfire, simply refused to dogfight in the manner expected; any German pilot who tried it did not live very long. Frequently the fight would develop into a diving race, either trying to 'bounce' the other fellow from out of the sun, or else trying to get away after being 'bounced'. And with the early Spitfires as one neared 400mph the ailerons became heavier and heavier, until at 430mph the pilot needed all the strength of both hands to get about one tenth aileron movement. In an air combat this was a crippling defect: if one was diving on an enemy the idea was to fire at him on the way down, and the poor aileron control made this very difficult. At the time there was a terrific flap about it and my Handling Research Team at Farnborough had the job of helping to track down the cause. Luckily

the reason was found quite quickly: at high speeds the fabric covering of the ailerons ballooned out, so that the trailing edge became much thicker. Now the amount of stick force required to move a control surface is critically dependant upon the sharpness of the angle of the trailing edge of the surface and just a small increase in the angle can make a considerable difference to the force needed. The answer was to replace the fabric on the ailerons with light alloy, which did not balloon at high speeds. Vickers hastily knocked out a set of metal-covered ailerons and when these were fitted to the Spitfire there was a dramatic improvement in its high speed handling characteristics. During 1941 there was a large-scale retrospective modification programme to fit all the Spitfires with the new ailerons.

In war nothing stands still; the Germans and the Japanese improved their aircraft and so did we. The key to higher performance was a more powerful engine and Rolls Royce began to get more and more power first out of the Merlin and then out of the Griffon. The Spitfire began to carry progressively larger propellers, with four and later five blades, to absorb this extra power. Aerodynamically, such a propellor produced an effect on stability similar to that one would expect from a large cruciform fin on the nose, while the

94

Below: This Spitfire Mark IV, the only one built, was the first to be fitted with the Griffon engine; the latter was developed from the Merlin and was only a little larger externally, but it had a cubic capacity greater by more than a third. At the time this photograph was taken the aircraft was being used to test the mock-up of the proposed six-cannon installation for the Spitfire, and modified flaps.

Bottom: The Spitfire XII was the first Griffon-engined version to enter service; only one hundred were built, and the Mark XII went into service with Nos 41 and 91 Squadrons early in 1943. The Griffon rotated the propeller in the opposite direction to the Merlin; thus, instead of the accustomed swing to the left during take-off, the Griffon Spitfires swung strongly to the right. On one occasion a pilot took off in one of the new Spitfires without receiving a briefing on this important difference. As he lined-up for take-off he wound on full right rudder trim and put on a boot-full of right rudder to catch the expected fierce torque from the engine when it took effect. He pushed open the throttle and, with everything set the wrong way, the Spitfire swung viciously to the right like an unleashed animal; she finally got airborne at ninety degrees to the intended direction of take-off, narrowly missing a hangar in her path. It was a chastened and extremely attentive young man who landed the Spitfire a few minutes later, to learn the mysteries of the new version!

slipstream rotation tried to screw the machine into a roll; the rotating propeller would twist the air behind it so that it hit the fin and tailplane at an angle. These factors combined to produce unpleasant handling characteristics during the climb at full power: a great deal of twist and airflow on the side of the fin, trying to make the aircraft roll and yaw simultaneously, at a time when there was insufficient airspeed over the rudder for it to 'bite' properly. These effects tended to become more and more serious as the Spitfire progressed through its various marks, and had to be corrected by adding more area to the fin and rudder. For the most part the story of the aerodynamic development of the Spitfire was one of piling on more and more power transmitted through larger and larger propellers and the airframe designer having to tailor the rear end to compensate for this. Some of the very late versions of the Spitfire were fitted with the contra-rotating propeller, which was the only real solution to the problem; but these did not go into service until well after the end of the war and then in only small numbers.

I have mentioned some of the problems we had with the Spitfire, but with her thin wing she was able to cope with the greater engine powers and the higher speeds better than any other fighter of her vintage. The thickness-

chord ratio at the wing root of the Spitfire was only about 13 per cent, compared with 14.8 per cent for the Messerschmitt 109 and 16 per cent for the Hurricane; even the later Mustang, hailed as a very clean aeroplane, had a 16 per cent wing. After the first year of war there was a steady pressure on designers to increase the maximum permissable diving speed of the new fighters entering service, because this was one of the things the pilots really wanted for combat. As a result we soon found ourselves on the brink of the subsonic region, with shock waves beginning to form on the wing. Now on a fattish wing the shock waves begin to form quite early, at about .7 Mach (roughly 500mph at 20,000 feet, depending on temperature). As the aircraft neared the speed of sound the shock waves got stronger and on those wartime aircraft they would begin to upset the airflow over the wing, effect fore and aft stability, and cause all sorts

of unpleasant effects. One way to postpone the Mach effects is to use a swept-back wing; but another is to have a thinner wing and that is why we at Farnborough selected the Spitfire as one of the aircraft for the exploratory work on high speed dives. This series of trials began in May 1943, and during its course Squadron Leader 'Marty' Martindale managed to get a Spitfire XI diving at about .9 Mach[*]. This was a most remarkable effort for an aircraft designed in 1935 and I think I am right in saying that this speed was not exceeded until the Americans began their trials with the rocket-powered Bell X-1 in

[*]It must be stressed that to achieve such a high Mach number the Spitfire had to be taken straight down in a 45 degree dive, from 40,000 feet to about 20,000 feet. Thus the ability to reach such a high Mach number was unlikely to occur during a fighter-versus-fighter combat, though reconnaissance Spitfires were sometimes to use high speed dives to escape from enemy jet fighters (see page 132).

1948; certainly the RAF had nothing able to out-dive the Spitfire until the swept-wing F-86 Sabre came into service in 1951. It was during one of these high speed dives, in April 1944, while he was coming down at more than 600mph, that 'Marty' suffered a loss of oil pressure to the airscrew constant speed unit; the propeller simply went round faster and faster, taking the protesting engine with it, until the blades fractured and the engine shook itself to pieces. In masterly fashion he regained control and after a glide of some 20 miles he landed safely at Farnborough in his strained aircraft. The following month he was flying a replacement Spitfire in a further trial in the series, and again at a high Mach number he suffered a burst supercharger. This time the weather was bad and he eventually crash landed in a wood not far from the airfield; he managed to scramble clear of his burning aircraft on the ground then, in spite of spinal injuries, he returned to the wreck and retrieved the vital recording camera. For this he received a well-earned AFC.

Why was the Spitfire so good? I think it was because it had such a thin wing. Of course, Mitchell had been meticulous in his attention to detail in the design of the Spitfire; but basically the reason for her ability to remain in the forefront of the technological race for so long was the fact that she had a wing thinner than that of any of her contemporaries. Considering that he could have had little knowledge of Mach effects, Mitchell's decision to use such a thin wing was not only bold but inspired. We now know that it was a close run thing: had he made the wing just a little thinner it would probably have been too weak, and aileron reversal would have been encountered lower down the speed scale. And if that had happened, the Spitfire would have been just one more of those aircraft that did not quite make the grade.

In a long war of attrition, repair was just as important as production.

Left: the large Spitfire salvage section at the overhaul and repair factory of Air Service Training at Hamble.

Top, Above: this seemingly ruined Mark XII, which had belonged to No 91 Squadron, was actually repaired at Hamble and put back in service.

Equal to the Very Best

The Mark XIV was the most potent version of the Spitfire to enter large-scale service before the end of the Second World War. In the spring of 1944 No 610 Squadron became operational with the Mark, eight years after the prototype Spitfire made her initial flight and five and a half years after the first Mark Is entered service. How did the Spitfire XIV stand in 1944, in comparison with other modern fighters in the Royal Air Force, the US Army Air Force and the *Luftwaffe?* Fortunately we know in some detail, for early in 1944 the Air Fighting Development Unit ran a trial to compare her with the Tempest V, the Mustang III (P-51B), the Focke Wulf 190A and the Messerschmitt 109G; had he lived to read the report, Reginald Mitchell would have had little reason to feel humble . . .

Brief Tactical Comparison with the Tempest V

Range and Endurance Rough comparisons have been made at the maximum cruising conditions of both aircraft. It is interesting that the indicated airspeed of each is about 280mph and the range of each is about identical; both with full fuel load (including long-range tanks) and without.

Maximum Speed From 0-10,000 feet the Tempest V is 20mph faster than the Spitfire XIV. There is then little to choose until 22,000 feet, when the Spitfire XIV becomes 30-40mph faster, the Tempest's operational ceiling being about 30,000 feet as opposed to the Spitfire XIV's 40,000 feet.

Maximum Climb The Tempest is not in the same class as the Spitfire XIV. The Tempest V, however, has a considerably better zoom climb, holding a higher

Below: A section of Spitfire XIVs of No 610 Squadron, the first unit to receive this version. The aircraft nearest the camera was piloted by the squadron commander, Squadron Leader R. Newbury.

speed throughout the manoeuvre. If the climb is prolonged until climbing speed is reached then, of course, the Spitfire XIV will begin to catch up and pull ahead.

Dive The Tempest V gains on the Spitfire XIV.

Turning Circle The Spitfire XIV easily out-turns the Tempest.

Rate of Roll The Spitfire XIV rolls faster at speeds below 300mph, but definitely more slowly at speeds greater than 350mph.

Conclusions The tactical attributes of the two aircraft being completely different, they require a separate handling technique in combat. For this reason, Typhoon squadrons should convert to Tempests, and Spitfire squadrons to Spitfire XIVs, and definitely never vice-versa, or each aircraft's particular advantages would not be appreciated. Regarding performance, if correctly handled, the Tempest is better below about 20,000 feet and the Spitfire XIV is better above that height.

Tactical Comparison with the Mustang III

Radius of Action Without a long-range tank, the Spitfire XIV has no endurance compared with the Mustang. With a 90 gallon long-range tank it has about half the range of the Mustang III fitted with two 62½ gallon long-range tanks.

Maximum Speed The maximum speeds are practically identical.

Maximum Climb The Spitfire XIV is very much better.

Dive The Mustang pulls away.

Turning Circle The Spitfire XIV is the better.

Rate of Roll. The advantage tends to be with the Spitfire XIV.

Conclusion With the exception of endurance, no conclusions should be drawn as these two aircraft should never be enemies. The choice is a matter of taste.

Combat Trial Against the Fw 190A

Maximum Speeds From 0-5,000ft and 15,000-20,000ft the Spitfire XIV is only

Below: The first Mark I Spitfires to be delivered carried no armour; but it was not long before steel plating to the rear of the pilot's seat, and a toughened glass windscreen, became standard. The armour fitted to the Spitfire Mark XIV was typical of that in a western fighter of the late war period; it was designed to protect the pilot against German Mauser 20mm armour-piercing rounds fired at medium ranges from the rear 20 degree cone and German 13mm rounds fire from the forward 20 degree cone (the former from attacking fighters, the latter from defending bombers). Although it suffered in the process, the engine also afforded the pilot considerable protection against rounds fired from ahead.

Light Alloy: 8 SWG – approx 4 mm   10 SWG – approx 3 mm

Armour Plate: 7mm   6mm   4mm

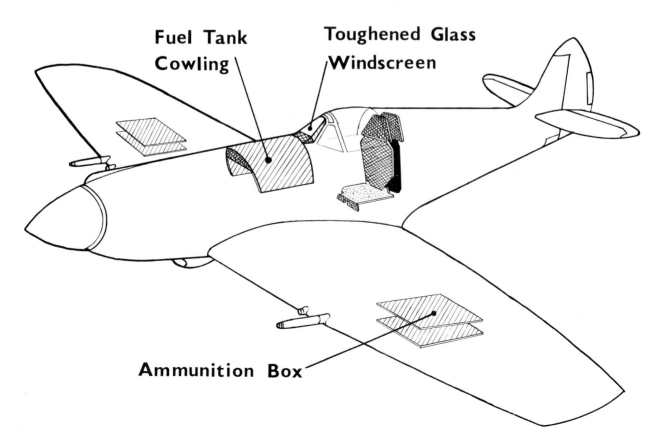

Fuel Tank Cowling   Toughened Glass Windscreen

Ammunition Box

20mph faster; at all other heights it is up to 60mph faster than the Fw 190A. It is estimated to have about the same maximum speed as the new Fw 190 (DB 603) at all heights*.

Maximum Climb The Spitfire XIV has a considerably greater rate of climb than the Fw 190A or (estimated) the new Fw 190 (DB 603) at all heights.

Dive After the initial part of the dive, during which the Fw 190 gains slightly, the Spitfire XIV has a slight advantage.

Turning Circle The Spitfire XIV can easily turn inside the Fw 190. Though in the case of a right-hand turn, this difference is not quite so pronounced.

Rate of Roll The Fw 190 is very much better.

Conclusions In defence, the Spitfire XIV should use its remarkable maximum climb and turning circle against any enemy aircraft. In the attack it can afford to 'mix it' but should beware the quick roll and dive. If this manoeuvre is used by an Fw 190 and the Spitfire XIV follows, it will probably not be able to close the range until the Fw 190 has pulled out of its dive.

Combat Trial Against the Me 109G

Maximum Speed The Spitfire XIV is 40mph faster at all heights except near 16,000ft, where it is only 10mph faster.

Maximum Climb. The same result: at 16,000ft the two aircraft are identical, otherwise the Spitfire XIV out-climbs the Me 109G. The zoom climb is practically identical when the climb is made without opening the throttle. Climbing at full throttle, the Spitfire XIV draws away from the Me 109G quite easily.

Dive During the initial part of the dive, the Me 109G pulls away slightly, but when a speed of 380mph is reached, the Spitfire XIV begins to gain on the Me 109G.

Turning Circle The Spitfire XIV easily out-turns the Me 109G in either direction.

Rate of Roll The Spitfire XIV rolls much more quickly.

Conclusion The Spitfire XIV is superior to the Me 109G in every respect.

Combat Performance with 90 Gallon Long-Range Tanks

As the Spitfire XIV has a very short range it has been assumed that when a long-range tank is to be carried, it is most likely to be the 90 gallon tank rather than the 30 gallon or 45 gallon. Pending further instructions, no drops or trials have been carried out with the 30 gallon or the 45 gallon tanks. The aircraft's performance with either can be estimated from the results given below of trials with the 90 gallon long-range tank.

Drops The aircraft was fitted with assistor springs as for the Spitfire IX. Two drops were made with empty tanks at 50ft and 25,000ft, 250mph IAS, with no real trouble. Cine photographs were taken and show the tank dropping quite clear of the aircraft. Further trials would be necessary to check these results thoroughly.

Speeds About 20mph is knocked off the maximum speed and correspondingly off the speed at intermediate throttle settings. The aircraft is then still faster than the Fw 190A and the Me 109G above 20,000 feet.

Climb Climb is most effected. With a half-full tank its maximum climb becomes identical with the Spitfire IX without the tank. Even with a full tank it can therefore climb as fast as the Fw 190A or the Me 109G. Its zoom climb is hardly effected.

Dive So long as the tank is more than one-third full, the dive acceleration is similar.

Turning Circle The Spitfire XIV now has a definitely wider turning circle than before, but it is still within those of the Fw 190A and the Me 109G.

Rate of Roll Similar to that when no tank is fitted.

Conclusions Even with a 90 gallon long-range tank, the Spitfire XIV can equal or outclass the Fw 190A and the Me 109G in every respect. Its main advantages remain the tight turn and the maximum climb.

*This is a reference to the 'D' version of the Fw 190, fitted with the more powerful Daimler Benz 603 motor, whose appearance had long been predicted by Allied air intelligence; in fact, the first Fw 190Ds were not encountered in combat until late in the summer of 1944.

The Second Greatest Thrill a Man Can Have

Frank Hercliffe

A Seafire with a trainee pilot about to touch down on the short deck of the escort carrier HMS Ravager Lieutenant Astin was on the bats, while Lieutenant Cunningham maintained a strong professional interest in the proceedings.

Right: As she approached to land on HMS Attacker this Seafire L.11c of 879 squadron went too low; note the raised arms of the batsman, behind the screen, telling the pilot he must go up.

Centre Right: The pilot applied power to clear the edge of the deck but overdid it, and began to increase his speed. He was now in the wrong attitude to take a wire and bounced over all of them . . .

Below right: . . . going full-tilt into the barrier . . .

Bottom right: . . . before finally coming to rest in the forward deck park after smashing the tail of a stationary Seafire.

Far right: The Seafire was judged a write-off and, after everything useful had been stripped from her, axes were used to smash the wings and fuselage to ensure that when dumped the wreckage would sink rapidly.

Below far right: Carefully the wreckage was lowered into the water, lest it should sink too quickly and foul the ship's screw or rudder.

The landing of any sort of fixed-winged aircraft on the deck of a ship requires flying skill of a high order. But to land a Seafire on the short flight deck of an escort carrier was particularly difficult, for there was little margin for error.

Above: When the remains were well clear the line was let slip, and another Seafire was consigned to 'the greatest dustbin in the world'.

Having completed almost a hundred hours flying time in the Seafire and made scores of aerodrome dummy deck landings at the Naval Air Station at Henstridge in Somerset, as a young Sub-lieutenant I was judged to be ready for my first landing on a carrier at sea. Accordingly I took off from the Naval Air Station at Ayr one fine summer's day and made off north-eastwards at 3,000 feet towards the training carrier *HMS Ravager,* which was cruising off the Isle of Arran. A few minutes after take-off I caught sight of her — or rather her wake — as she pushed herself through the water at about 20 knots. From the air she looked ridiculously small. Could I *really* land on that?

Over the radio I received clearance to join the carrier's circuit; and once I was down at 500 feet she did look a little bigger — though still too small for my liking. Quickly I ran through my pre-landing checks: wheels, flaps and hook down, mixture rich and propeller in fine pitch. Then I pulled my harness

Below: Flying accidents were not the sole hazard to aircraft, life and limb on an aircraft carrier. During the night of August 6th 1943 the escort carrier HMS Hunter, carying the Seafires of Nos 899 and 834 Squadrons, ran into a gale in the Bay of Biscay. One of the Seafires had not been lashed down securely enough and broke free. Defying all attempts by the ship's crew to secure her, she smashed into the next aircraft and cut her free also. The process continued and within a short time the hangar was filled with Seafires sliding up and down the deck as the ship rolled and pitched, bent on destroying themselves and all around them. These photographs, showing Hunter's hangar as it looked on August 7th, convey the scene of utter chaos and destruction. The Seafires were of the 11C version, which lacked provision for wing folding.

Seafires pictured with some of the more exotic naval loads: Top with the Mine 'A' Mark VIII, which weighed 500 pounds; Centre: with two 200 pound smoke floats; and Above with the 250 pound 'B' bomb. The 'B' (or buoyant) Bomb had a hollow nose section, and was designed to attack moving armoured warships from underneath. Released into the water ahead of the target ship, the bomb's momentum took it to a depth of about 50 feet before it up-ended and floated nose-first to the surface; on the way up it would (hopefully) be 'run-over' by the ship and explode against the thin bottom plating. Great things had been expected from this weapon prior to the war and it was issued to several RAF and Fleet Air Arm squadrons; but the problem of accurate aiming was never solved and the 'B' bomb was rarely and never successfully used on operations.

Right: A Seafire III, showing the method of wing folding introduced with this version.

tight, pulled down my goggles, and slid back the hood. The view over the nose of the Seafire was notoriously bad and the only way to put one down on the deck was to fly a curved approach to enable one to keep the carrier in sight throughout. I began my run in from a position about half a mile off *Ravager's* port quarter, with my head out the port side of the cockpit watching the antics of the batsman on the port side of the carrier.

During the final approach I knew I had to follow the batsman's instructions implicitly; since my own head was outside the cockpit I had no idea what my instruments were reading and I had to rely on him to bring me in. But the batsmen were all very experienced deck landing pilots themselves and they knew their business; merely by observing the attitude of the Seafire, they could judge her speed to within 2 or 3 knots. That final approach took well under a minute, but at the time it felt like a lifetime: nose well up, plenty of power on and the deck getting progressively larger and larger. The batsman's signals told me I was doing all right: down a bit . . . down a bit . . . OK . . . OK . . . Suddenly his left forearm went horizontally across his chest: cut! I yanked back the throttle and for an instant everything seemed to go quiet. Then the hook caught the No 2 wire, my Seafire was plucked from the sky and the wheels hit the deck with a thump. Firmly I was drawn to a halt and, thanks to my tightened straps, I had no feeling of violent deceleration. I was down!

Almost at once people seemed to emerge from holes all round the deck. The Deck Control Officer ran out to a position in front of my starboard wing, two seamen ran out clutching chocks and made for my wheels, and through the corner of my eye I could see others struggling to clear my hook from the wire and lock it in the 'up' position under the fuselage. The next thing I knew, the DCO was waving his flag above his head: the signal for me to rev. up the engine for an immediate take off. I was much too busy for any self-congratulations, which was probably just as well.

The take-off from a carrier was straight forward, though it did involve a bit of juggling immediately afterwards. Because of the risk of ditching we always launched with our canopies open and the door catches on half-cock so that we could get them open quickly if we had to make a hurried exit. For the actual take-off we held the stick in the right hand and the throttle in the left. Then, as soon as we were airborne, we had to change hands and take the stick in the left, so that we could retract the undercarriage with the lever on our right. That done we had to change hands again, controlling the Seafire with the right hand while closing fully the door with our left. Then we changed hands yet again, holding the stick in the left hand while sliding forward the canopy with our right. After that a final change of hands, to enable us to press the throttle-mounted transmit button and announce to the world that we were safely airborne. At the end of it all, I knew how the proverbial one-armed paper-hanger must have felt!

That first day I did eight landings, with a break for coffee in the middle; my third was a bit hairey, when I took No 7 out of the eight wires — had I taken the 8th, I should also have hit the barrier. So it was that I had my initiation into the realities of landing a Seafire on the deck of an escort carrier — the second greatest thrill a man can have.

Gunfire Spotter
Captain Dick Law, CBE DSC RN (Retired)

Versatility was one of the most important assets possessed by the Spitfire, and during the Second World War she was employed on a range of tasks which probably went far beyond Reginald Mitchell's wildest dreams for his beautiful little fighter. One such was that of spotting for the heavy naval guns which played such an important part during the invasion of Normandy.

In March 1944 I was a Lieutenant serving as the Senior Pilot of No 886 Squadron, equipped with the Seafire L III. It was then that we learned that our role in the forthcoming invasion was to be that of gunfire spotters for the bombarding battleships, cruisers and monitors. Our targets were to be the German coastal batteries, with their large calibre guns set in massive concrete emplacements, positioned to cover all possible landing areas along the northern coast of France.

The importance of our spotting role was drilled into us from the beginning and there was no feeling that we, as fighter pilots, were to be missemployed during the great invasion. Only heavy naval gunfire, corrected from the air and sustained for a period of days if need be, could neutralise these powerful defensive positions during the critical period while our troops fought their way ashore: low level bombing would have been too costly, high level bombing would have been too inaccurate and neither type of bombing could have brought speedy retaliation against the new batteries the Germans were almost certain to bring up.

Gradually we learnt the mechanics of bringing heavy gunfire to bear on a target; first on a sand table, then with a

Lieutenant Dick Law bringing his Seafire close alongside the photographic aircraft. The Seafire, serial MB 328, was the first machine in the batch of forty-eight Mark IBs which had been converted from Mark V Spitfires in mid-1942, by Air Services Training.

Above: Dick Law, pictured after the war when he held the rank of Commander.

gunfire spotting it was usual for our Seafires to fly in pairs, with one correcting the fire and the other standing off a couple of thousand feet above keeping watch for any enemy fighters which might attempt to interfere.

The first target we were to engage was the battery at Villerville near Trouville, where there were six 155mm guns in a heavily concreted position. When I was ready, the carefully-rehearsed patter began. I called up *Warspite* on the VHF and told her "Target located, ready to open fire". She gave me a call five seconds before opening fire, then as she fired she called "Shot" followed by a figure, say "52"; the figure gave the predicted time of flight of the shells — just over fifty seconds for the firing range of fifteen miles. The battleship was a magnificent sight as she lay at anchor, loosing off four-gun salvoes with her main 15-inch guns. On the call "Shot" I started my stop-watch and headed inland, so as to have the target in clear view when the shells impacted. As they burst I would radio back a correction to bring the fire directly on to the target, say "Left 100, up 400", the distances being measured in yards. While the ship's gunners were reloading I would head back over the sea; there was no point in hanging around over enemy territory and risking being shot down and jeopardizing the whole operation, for no useful purpose.

When *Warspite* indicated that she was ready to fire again, I would move into position to observe the target and the process would be repeated.

During one of the early salvoes I was a little over-enthusiastic in positioning myself to observe the fall of the shells, with the result that some thirty-five seconds after *Warspite* had fired my Seafire suddenly shivered and I actually saw one of the giant shells, weighing almost a ton, go sizzling close past me on its way to the target. During subsequent salvoes, I made good and sure that I was well to the side of the line of fire!

From time to time the German batteries attempted to return *Warspite's* fire; when that happened we were

troop of 25 pounders on an army gunnery range and finally with a cruiser firing off the coast of Scotland. Near the end of May we moved to our operational base for the invasion, at Lee on Solent; the great event, for which we had all trained so hard, was close at hand.

On the actual day of the invasion, June 6th, I was up very early and with my wingman I arrived over Normandy soon after 0600 hours to take control of the guns of the battleship *HMS Warspite*. I should mention that for treated to the spectacle of a giant-sized tennis match. During one of these exchanges a salvo straddled *Warspite,* but she received only slight damage.

After about forty minutes of spotting my fuel was beginning to run low, and after being relieved by two more Seafires we returned to Lee. We spotted for *Warspite* during two further sorties that day.

On the second day of the invasion, June 7th, we were detailed to spot for American warships on the western flank of the bridgehead; accordingly, I found myself controlling the gunfire of the battleship *USS Nevada.* The shoot went according to plan and when the relieving Seafires arrived both my wingman and I had some fuel to spare; so we decided to seek out a 'target of opportunity' (anything on the ground that looked vaguely German) and shoot it up before going home.

The decision, casually made, nearly proved fatal for me. Looking back on that part of the sortie, I can see now that we were both grossly overconfident about the success of the invasion. We had been keyed-up for a ding-dong battle with the *Luftwaffe;* but the enemy air force had simply failed to show up and from our lofty viewpoint it appeared that the whole thing was becoming a walk-over. Now we felt that we could hardly go home without having played some more direct part in the impending collapse of the Third Reich. Below us we saw an enemy gun position and we decided that we would wipe it off the face of the earth. It was not, however, a very professional attack; confident in our superiority we took our time turning in and lining up and the men on the ground could have had no doubts regarding our intentions. Unfortunately for us the guns were 37mm *Flak,* manned by crews who certainly did not share our feelings regarding the hopelessness of their cause. As we ran in they were ready and their first few rounds of tracer were extremely accurate: I heard a rapid 'plunk plunk' as a couple of the shells exploded against my aircraft. It was immediately apparent that they had hit my radiator,

for almost at once my engine temperature guage needle began to climb steadily until finally it was hard against the upper stop. Simultaneously I caught the unmistakable stench of vapourized glycol and the engine coughed to a stop.

I pointed the Seafire's nose towards the coast as I pulled up, but it soon became clear that I had insufficient height to reach the sea; I selected some flat land a little way inland and prepared to put her down there. The actual belly landing was a bit of an anti-climax: the Seafire slid gently to a halt on the soft marshland and there was no fire or drama of any sort.

As I clambered out of the aircraft I rapidly became aware of the appalling din of battle: there seemed to be guns of all calibres firing and shells exploding — the latter, fortunately, all some distance away. In the cockpit of my noisy aircraft far above, I had been quite oblivious to the intensity of the battle below.

Then the rushes in front of me parted, and there was a very tall American negro Corporal who beckoned me over. Apparently, I had come down in an uncontested part of no-man's-land. When I reached him his first gesture was to offer me a swig from his water bottle; I was not all that thirsty at the time but I thought it good manners to accept — and I was glad I did, for the bottle contained a very reasonable vin rose. I later learned that he had been ashore only a few hours, so he must have been a pretty good organiser!

Gradually I worked my way back through the system to the beach, where I was taken out to a motor torpedo boat which took me back to England. I was soon able to rejoin my squadron and, after my salutary experience, contented myself with betting bigger guns than my Seafire's to do the work of destruction.

The success of the Normandy landings and their effect on the course of the war, are now common knowledge. Without doubt the accuracy of the heavy naval gunfire played a major part in making this possible, and I am very happy that I was able to assist in this.

Achtung! Jabo!

German motor transport burning in Normandy, after a fighter-bomber attack.

With the Luftwaffe able to mount only spasmodic operations over Normandy after the invasion, the Allied fighters were able to concentrate their efforts against the enemy ground forces. Achtung! Jabo! (Look out! Fighter-bomber!) became a shout to strike fear in the hearts of the German soldiers. Although tests had been carried out, the Spitfires did not carry rockets during this battle, but they were no less effective against the German armour for that. In fact it was the lack of fuel, due to the aerial interdiction of supplies, which crippled the Panzer Divisions in Normandy and not, as many sources have stated, the attacks by rocket-firing fighters. After the Falaise battle operational research teams from the British 21st Army Group combed the area and found a total of three hundred abandoned German tanks and self-propelled guns (almost sufficient to equip two Panzer Divisions). Of these only eleven (less than 4 per cent) had been knocked out by rockets. Fifty-four had been abandoned for miscellaneous reasons (mechanical breakdown, etc) and two had been knocked out by bombs. The remaining 233 (77 per cent) were undamaged or else had been destroyed by German demolition charges; lacking fuel, they could not move when the German army began its headlong retreat. The persistent strafing attacks on the

German columns of soft-skinned supply vehicles, by Spitfires and other Allied fighters using cannon and machine-guns, played a major part in creating the conditions for the victory on the ground. These German photographs, taken during the battle, provide an interesting insight into conditions on the other side of the battle line:

Top: a Spitfire seen pulling

up after a strafing run;

Above: Jabofalle (fighter-bomber-trap), a heavily camouflaged quadruple-barrelled 20mm Flak gun, awaiting an enemy to be lured into range by a tempting target nearby;

Topcentre: a German soldier standing guard over a Spitfire of No 602 Squadron which had been shot down over Normandy.

Above: A high-altitude variant like the Mark VI, the Mark VII was powered by the more powerful Merlin 61 engine. Although many of the Mark VIIs were fitted with the pointed wing tips it can be seen that this example, which belonged to No 131 Squadron, had normal eliptical tips. No 131 Squadron received its Mark VIIs in March 1944 and, at the time this photograph was taken, provided bomber escorts after the Normandy invasion, and also operated in the ground-attack role.

Left: Engine-change de-lux: fitters of No 442 Squadron RCAF doing an engine change in the field, with the luxury of a mobile crane to the hard work. If no such crane was available ground crews had to use a set of wooden shear legs with a block and tackle to hoist the engine out, then push the Spitfire clear before lowering the engine on to a trolley; refitting was the same process, in reverse. During the campaigns in North Africa, Italy, France and the Far East, the great majority of Spitfire servicing had to be done in the open where, as one fitter commented: "If it rained that was just tough luck—both you and the Spitfire got wet!"

Left: A close-up of the so-called 'Depth Charge Modification XXX', to enable the Spitfire to transport a pair of containers with a beverage in great demand in Normandy. The Spitfire was not cleared for the full range of combat manoeuvers while operating in this configuration.

Spitfire v Doodle Bug

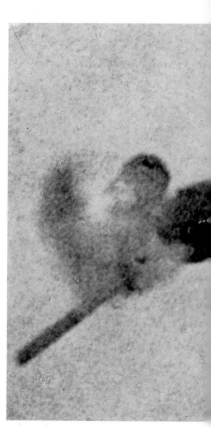

Left: One way to bring down a V 1, without risking detonating the warhead, was to topple its gyro-stabilisation mechanism by tipping up a wing; the V 1 had no ailerons and was therefore particularly vulnerable to interference in the rolling plain. Some pilots achieved the tipping by the 'brute force' method of using their own wing to knock up that of the flying-bomb; but since the V 1s were skinned in rolled steel and the wing tips of the fighters were constructed from far weaker light alloy, this method was not without hazards of its own. A rather neater method was to make use of simple aerodynamics, to achieve the same end without actually coming into physical contact with the bomb . . .

Far right: (1) the Spitfire pilot positioned his wing close over that of the V 1, thus destroying the lift on that side . . . (2) and the flying-bomb's wing dropped. The fighter remained in position causing the missile to increase its angle of bank until the crude stabilisation system could no longer cope and . . . (3 and 4) it fell out of control and the Spitfire pulled clear.

Right: An ever-present danger if attacks on V 1s were pressed to short range was that the warhead, containing nearly 1,900 pounds of high explosive, would detonate. Flight Lieutenant G. Armstrong of No 165 Squadron brought back this 'toasted' Spitfire IX after a rather-too-exciting tussle with a V 1 on July 1st.

114

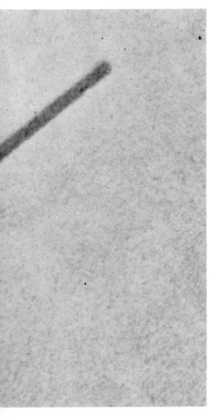

Left: In June 1944 the Germans opened their long-expected bombardment of London using V 1 flying-bombs. Although it flew straight and level, the V 1 was not an easy target to shoot down. The speeds at which these missiles flew varied greatly, with the slowest coming in at about 300mph and the fastest recorded at 440mph; thus while the slower missiles were comparatively easy for fighters to catch, the fastest outran all except the Spitfire XIVs and Tempest Vs. Moreover, since the flying-bombs were constructed mainly from sheet steel, they were less vulnerable to cannon and machine-gun fire than were normal manned aircraft. This photograph shows a V 1 receiving a strike from a 20mm explosive shell, fired from the starboard quarter.

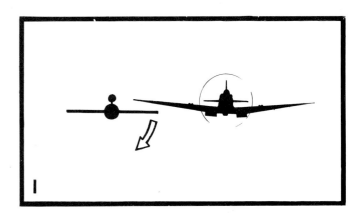

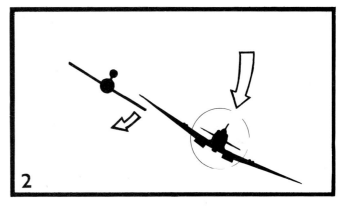

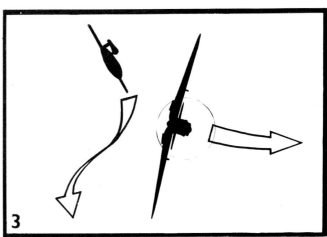

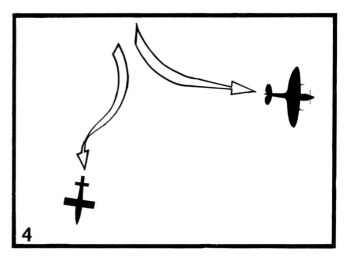

Foe Without Mercy
Wing Commander 'Hank' Costain, MBE

In spite of the advances made in aviation, man is allowed to use the sky on sufferance, never as a right; and, as 'Hank' Costain now tells us, the elements can regain control of their domain in most brutal fashion.

During the summer of 1944 I was a Flying Officer with No 615 Squadron, operating Spitfire VIIIs. During the battle to repel the attempted Japanese invasion of India we had been flying from Palel on the Imphal Plain; but the time came for us to pull back out of the front line for a brief rest. Accordingly on August 10th our sixteen aircraft took off from Palel with the CO in the lead, for a nice easy trip back to Baigachi near Calcutta; for a quarter of the pilots, however, the flight would be their last.

For much of the route we had underneath us puffs of thin fair-weather cumulus, and as we neared our destination we let down through them. Soon afterwards the cloud cover above us became complete, but as we had good contact with the ground everything seemed all right. Indeed it was, until straddling our path we found a thick brown storm cloud extending right down to the ground. Clearly we could

Above: Wing Commander 'Hank Costain.

Right: Hank Costain with one of the Mark VIII Spitfires of No 615 Squadron, at readiness at Palel in June 1944.

not go forwards through it and, because we had passed our point of no return, we could not go back to Palel either. So the CO decided to take us back a little way, then we could climb up through the layer of cumulus and once above it we could search for a way through the storm. But it never happened that way.

Soon after re-entering cloud there was a sudden bang, and everything seemed to happen at once: the sky turned black as pitch, my Spitfire reared up and the stick seemed to go wild in its attempts to wrench itself out of my grasp. Somehow we had slid into that dreadfully turbulent monsoon storm cloud. Within seconds I was completely out of control and with the artificial horizon toppled I had not the faintest idea which way was 'up'. Outside it was so dark that I could not even see my wing tips and the pounding of the walnut-sized hailstones on the fuselage drowned even the noise of the engine. In my earphones I heard the frenzied chatter of the other pilots as they tried to fight their way free from the storm's clutches.

Of my flight instruments only the altimeter seemed to be reading correctly, and from its spinning needles I learned that I was in a violent up-current. After going up rapidly

through nearly ten thousand feet, during which my stick seemed to have no effect at all, the Spitfire bucked and entered an equally-vicious down-draft and we were plunging earthwards just as fast. I was terrified. Again, nothing I did with my controls seemed to make the slightest difference. As the altimeter reading neared 1,000 feet it became clear that this was no place for Mrs Costain's young lad. I had to bail out.

First I had to get rid of the hood, so I yanked hard on the jettison ball above my head; but the tropical heat had perished the rubber and it came away in my hand. Charming! Since the hood would not jettison I slid it fully back on its runners, then trimmed the nose fully down and undid my seat harness. Finally I let go of the stick and, as the Spitfire bunted forwards, up I went like a cork out of a bottle. At least I would have done, but not my parachute pack caught on the overhanging lip of the hood. The next thing I knew I was tumbling head-over-heels along the fuselage before ramming hard into the tailplane and shattering my leg. As the tail disappeared into the gloom I grabbed at the parachute 'D' ring and pulled it, then I glanced down to see the ground rushing up to meet me.

The canopy developed just in time, but even so the landing on my fractured leg was excruciatingly painful. As I lay in a sodden heap in that flooded Indian paddy field and began to collect my wits, my first thoughts were for the perfectly good Spitfire I had just abandoned. "Good God", I remember thinking, "What on earth am I going to tell the CO?" Luckily I was picked up by some of the locals soon afterwards and they took me to a doctor.

In less than five minutes No 615 Squadron had lost its commander and three other pilots killed and three more including myself injured; we had written-off half of our aircraft, eight of the most modern fighters in the theatre. And it had all happened without there being a Jap within a hundred miles. When it is angry, the sky is a foe without mercy.

Above: The captured
Japanese Mitsubishi A6M5
Zero-Sen fighter, Allied
code-name Zeke 52, which
flew in the comparative
performance trial against
the Seafire L IIC at the US
Navy test centre, Patuxent
River, in October, 1944.

In October 1944 Lieutenant Dick Law was sent to the US Naval Air Station at Patuxent River, Maryland, for a most interesting assignment: to take part in a comparative performance trial between the Seafire LIIC and a captured Zeke 52 — an improved version of the famous Zero fighter. Reproduced below are the conclusions drawn from the trial.

Results of Trials
The peak speeds of the two aircraft are:-
Seafire LIIC — 338mph at 5,500ft
Zeke 52 — 335mph at 18,000ft
The comparative speeds in miles per hour are:

Height	Seafire LIIC	Zeke 52
Sea Level	316	292
5,000ft	337	313
10,000ft	337	319
15,000ft	335	327
20,000ft	328	333
25,000ft	317	327
30,000ft	—	317

Climb the Zeke 52 climbs at a very steep angle and gives the impression of a very high rate of climb. The Seafire LIIC, however, has a much better initial climb and remains slightly superior up to 25,000ft.

The climb of the Seafire is at a higher speed, but at a more shallow angle.

The best indicated climbing speeds of the Zeke and the Seafire are 120mph and 160mph respectively.

Manoeuverability Turning plane — the Zeke 52 can turn inside the Seafire LIIC at all heights. The Zeke 52 turns tighter to the left than to the right.

Rolling plane — the rate of roll of the two aircraft is similar at speeds below 180mph IAS, but above that the aileron stick forces of the Zeke increase tremendously, and the Seafire becomes progressively superior.

Dive The Seafire is superior in the dive although initial acceleration is similar. The Zeke is a most unpleasant aircraft in a dive, due to heavy stick forces and excessive vibration.

Tactics: Never dogfight with the Zeke 52 — it is too manoeuerable.

At low altitudes where the Seafire is at its best, it should make use of its superior rate of climb and speed to obtain a height advantage before attacking.

If jumped, the Seafire should evade by using superior rate of roll. The Zeke cannot follow high speed rolls and aileron turns.

Conclusions The Seafire LIIC is 24 mph faster at sea level, this difference decreasing to parity between 15,000 and 20,000ft. The Zeke 52 is 10mph faster at 25,000ft.

The Seafire can out-climb the Zeke up to 25,000ft.

The Zeke is very manoeuverable and can turn inside the Seafire at all altitudes.

The Zeke fights best between 115 and 180mph IAS.

The rate of roll of the Seafire is better than that of the Zeke above 180mph IAS.

The Quest for Range

Right, Top right: Towards the end of 1943 the Flight Refuelling Company worked out a method of towing a Spitfire from a multi-engined bomber, as a means of extending the ferry range of the former; during the subsequent trials, a Wellington acted as tug. The towing line consisted of a 'Y' shaped bridle, with forked ends for attachment to the Spitfire's wings outside the propeller disc. For take-off the apex of the bridle was held by a quick-release catch to the underside of the rear fuselage of the Spitfire; this held the bridle clear of the propeller and under-carriage, preventing entangling when the Spitfire took off under her own power alongside the towing aircraft. The two aircraft climbed to their cruising altitude, where the Spitfire pilot released the bridle apex and the rest of the 700 foot long towline was paid out from the tug. The Spitfire then slowed down gradually until the line was taught, when the former's engine could be shut down. Flight trials soon proved that the towing scheme was not, however, as simple as it appeared. In a report dated February 1944 Captain Leslie Greensted, who piloted the Spitfire, highlighted the problems. Initially, the most serious was that if the Spitfire's Merlin engine was shut down or run at low speeds, it was liable to oil up; if, on the other hand, the throttle was opened sufficiently to prevent this, the Spitfire overtook the tug! To overcome this a fully-feathering airscrew was fitted—the only occasion a Spitfire was fitted with one—and the engine could be kept warm without producing excessive thrust. Other problems stemmed from the poor forward view from the Spitfire. During the spring of 1944, the towed Spitfire trials were abandoned.

Right: The first serious attempt to increase the range and endurance of the Spitfire came in the summer of 1940, when Mark I serial number P 9565 was modified to carry a fixed extra 30 gallon tank under the port wing. The handling characteristics of this aircraft were poor, however, and the report on the project stated that at an indicated airspeed of 350mph the ailerons became very heavy and 'considerable force' was needed to hold up the port wing. The following year a Mark II with metal ailerons was fitted with a similar fixed tank of 40 gallons capacity; in this form the modified Spitfire was judged suitable for service use, and was employed on operations during the latter half of 1941 by Nos 66, 118 and 152 Squadrons.

Right: The fixed extra wing tank did not find general favour, and was soon overtaken by the under-fuselage slipper tank which came in 30, 45, 90 and 170 gallon sizes. The last named, seen here, trebled the fuel capacity of the Spitfire V and made it possible for these aircraft to be flown to Malta direct from Gibraltar—a distance of nearly 1,200 miles. In this configuration the Spitfire V had a maximum still-air range of 1,450 miles, broken down as follows: climb and cruise for 940 miles using the fuel from the drop tank, at 170mph with a consumption of just over 5 miles per gallon; release the empty tank and cruise on the internal tank for 510 miles at 150 mph, with a consumption of just over 8 miles per gallon (from the point of view of range the lower speed was desirable in either configuration, but with the tank on at such a speed handling was difficult).

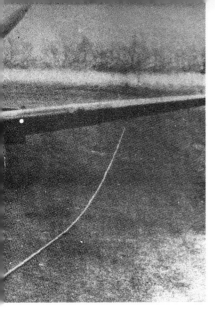

Right: Amongst the drop-tank configurations tested on the Spitfire was this one involving two 62 gallon tanks, one under each wing. Getting stores to fall away cleanly from an aircraft sometimes be a ticklish business, as can be seen from these series of photographs taken during the release trials for the 62 gallon tanks.

At 200mph (left line) the tank swung away from the Spitfire, but note that it held its position under the aircraft until after it had spun through a complete semi-circle; at one stage it was broadside-on to the airflow. At 250mph (centre line) the tank fell away cleanly. At 300mph the tail of the tank came up sharply and struck the underside of the wing, causing a severe dent (right line). The 62 gallon tank was not adopted for use on the Spitfire.

Spitfire Dive-Bomber
Raymond Baxter

Known to millions of television viewers for his popular science programme 'Tomorrow's World', Raymond Baxter spent most of the Second World War flying Spitfires. This section deals with his operational career during the final phase of the conflict.

In the autumn of 1944 I was a Flight Lieutenant commanding 'A' Flight of No 602 Squadron, with Squadron Leader Max Sutherland as my 'boss'. Prior to that I had flown Spitfires on operations almost continuously since the middle of 1941: in Britain with No 65 Squadron, then in the Mediterranean area with 93, and after that with No 602 Squadron during the Battle of Normandy. So by October 1944, when the squadron re-equipped with the Spitfire XVI and began re-training for the dive-bomber role, I was a fairly experienced operator.

In September 1944 the Germans began firing V2 rockets at London and the South East from launching sites in Holland. Together with the similarly equipped Nos 229, 453 and 603 Squadrons, we on 602 were given the task of maintaining vigorous patrol activity over the areas from which the

Above: Flight Lieutenant Raymond Baxter, second from the left, pictured briefing pilots of No 602 Squadron for an attack on a V2 target in Holland.

Below: American M10 three-tube cluster launchers, for 4.5-inch rockets, in a trial installation on a Spitfire IX.

rockets were coming, mainly round The Hague. If we saw any V2 activity on the ground we were, of course, to go in and sort it out. But the Germans were good at camouflage and it was unlike them to leave anything out in the open. So, to keep up the pressure, we were given a pretty wide-ranging brief. Since we knew that the Germans were very short of petrol at that stage, it was a safe assumption that any motor vehicle seen moving on the Dutch roads was doing something to assist the German war effort — it might even be associated with the V2 bombardment. Accordingly, we were given a free hand to 'shoot at anything that moved' — though naturally we went to great pains to avoid causing casualties to the Dutch civilian population.

In addition to our offensive patrols and interdiction sorties, we often carried out pre-planned dive-bombing attacks on suspected rocket storage areas and launching sites (the Dutch resistance organisation was particularly helpful in providing intelligence on these). Sometimes such a target would appear, from the air, as no more than a ring of wheel tracks on some scrubby heath land; even a careful study of aerial reconnaissance photographs often failed to reveal more.

The usual force to attack these small targets was four or six Spitfires, each loaded with either one 500 and two 250 pound bombs, or two 250 pounders and a long range tank. From our base at Coltishall, or its satellites at Ludham or Matlaske, we would head out across the North Sea climbing to about 8,000 feet. Once we made our landfall at the Dutch coast navigation was rarely a problem, because we quickly came to know our 'parish' like the backs of our hands. As we crossed into enemy territory we were liable to be engaged with predicted fire from heavy 88mm guns. But in a Spitfire this was no great danger, provided one continually changed one's direction and altitude in a series of long climbing or diving turns; if one did it right there was the immense satisfaction of seeing the black puffs of the shells going off where one would have been.

Generally the V2 targets were defended with light *Flak*, so when we reached the target area our approach tactics would vary. Sometimes we would go straight in and attack; other times we would dodge from cloud to cloud until we were in a favourable position, then go in; other times still we would overfly the target, then nip back from out of the sun to take the defenders by surprise. We were pretty wily birds!

Once we were committed to the dive-bombing attack, the procedure was usually standard. Running in at between 6,000 and 8,000 feet we would throttle back to just below 200mph, and aim to place the target so that it passed under the wing just inboard of the roundel. As it emerged from under the trailing edge we would roll over and pull the aircraft into a 70 degree dive — which felt vertical. At this stage one concentrated entirely on bringing the graticule of the gyro gunsight on to the target, ignoring the cockpit instruments and trying to ignore the *Flak*. Accurate bombing was dependant upon accurate flying during the dive and once the target was in the sight it was important to avoid side-slipping, skidding or turning for these would have induced errors. The Spitfires would go down in loose line astern, with 30 to 40 yards between aircraft and each pilot aiming and bombing individually. In a dive the speed would build up quite rapidly, to a maximum of about 360mph before the release. When he judged the altitude to be about 3,000 feet each pilot let go of his bombs in a salvo, then did a 5G pull-up to bring the nose up to the horizontal; by the time we had levelled out we were pretty low and the drill was to make a high speed getaway using the ground for cover. The great temptation was to pull up after attacking, to see how well one had done; but that could be fatal if the Germans were alert — and they usually were. We believed in going in tight, hitting hard, and getting the Hell out of it; there was no place for false heroics. The bombs we dropped were often fitted with delayed action fuses, some of them set to explode after as long as six hours; the object of the exercise was to make life difficult for the enemy for as long as possible.

During one of our attacks on a launching site we must have caught the V2 firing crew well into their count-down. After we had released our bombs and were going back for a low level 'strafe' with our cannon, one of the great flame-belching monsters began to climb slowly out from a clump of trees. Flight Sergeant 'Cupid' Love, one of my pilots,

actually fired a long burst at it with his cannon — which must have been the first ever attempt to bring down a ballistic missile in flight!

Sometimes we would mount set-piece attacks with other squadrons, if some particularly important target had been found. On March 18th 1944, for example, No 453 Squadron provided a diversion while we put in a six-aircraft strike at zero feet on the Baatasher-Mex office building in the middle of The Hague; we had had information that the missile firing experts were housed there. It was a very 'twitchy op', because we had to attack in close line abreast. All went well, however, and we wrecked the place. Max Sutherland received a bar to his DFC for that one — and had half of his starboard elevator shot away by *Flak*.

Often we flew two or even three sorties during a single day, with a landing at an airfield in Belgium between each to refuel and re-arm. On March 18th I flew three sorties: the first was a skip-bombing attack on a road bridge north of Gouda, the second was the raid on the Baatasher-Mex building, and the third was a low level interdiction sortie against the railway between Delft and Rotterdam.

All things considered, our losses during these attacks were light. And not all of them were due to enemy action; on at least one occasion a Spitfire shed its wings after the bombs had hung up at the end of the dive, and the pilot pulled up too hard. By this stage of the war, there was virtually nothing to be seen of the *Luftwaffe*.

Just how much our efforts contributed to the gradual run-down in the rate of firing V2s at England, I never did discover. But certainly it was all damned good fun for and unmarried 22 year old.

What did I think of the Spitfire? Every single one was different, with her own characteristics and foibles; if your own was unservicable and you took somebody else's, you could feel the difference at once. During the war I never wanted to operate in any other type of aircraft; the Spitfire was a darling little aeroplane.

Giving a rocket: although several different rocket installations were tried out, the RAF and the Royal Navy appear not to have used either the Spitfire or the Seafire to launch these missiles in action during the Second World War.

Far bottom right: four 3-inch rockets under the wing of a Seafire III, during a trial.

Below: the Triplex rocket, comprising three of the normal 3-inch rocket motors with a common combustion chamber, carried a 7.2-inch howitzer shell as warhead; it is seen here mounted on a Spitfire XVI.

Right: a pair of Triplex rockets being fired from a Spitfire.

Perhaps surprisingly, the Royal Hellenic Air Force was the first to employ rocket-firing Spitfires in action, when during December 1944 Mark IXs of No 336 Squadron Far right: fired these weapons at positions occupied by Communist rebels.

Hounded by Jets

For much of the war the unarmed photographic reconnaissance Spitfires had been able to go about their prying task without serious interference from the enemy. Flying fast, high and alone, they frequently came and went without any attempt being made to intercept them. During the closing months of the Second World War, however, there were ominous signs that the day of the uneventful reconnaissance sortie deep into Germany was fast drawing to a close; for the new jet fighters entering large-scale service in the *Luftwaffe,* the Messerschmitt 163 and the Messerschmitt 262, had the speed and the altitude performance to enable them to hack down the wide-ranging Spitfires. Typical of the brushes that resulted is this one which took place on March 7th 1945; the pilot, Flight Lieutenant Raby, was flying a Spitfire XI of No 542 Squadron.

On the morning of March 7, I was briefed to photograph the Bohlen Synthetic Oil Plant, the Molbis Thermal Power Station and the Oil Storage Depot at Rositz, all being to the south of Leipzig. A damage assessment was also required of Chemnitz which the RAF had attacked two days before.

At 0930 hours I took off carrying split 36-inch cameras with full magazines and all tanks full including a 90-gallon drop tank. I was soon well above cloud and heading out over the North Sea, eventually setting course at 35,000 feet. 10/10ths cloud lay well below and continued to within ten minutes of the target area. The trip was completely uneventful except for the disconcerting factor of the thick 100 yard non-persistent contrail I was trailing behind.

At 1125 hours I arrived in the area, Leipzig was clearly visible to the north and all my targets, including Chemnitz, in full view to the south east. Chemnitz lay under a thick pall of smoke which was drifting slowly to the south, otherwise little or no cloud was visible in the sky. I felt very visible to those on the

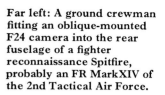

Far left: A ground crewman fitting an oblique-mounted F24 camera into the rear fuselage of a fighter reconnaissance Spitfire, probably an FR MarkXIV of the 2nd Tactical Air Force.

Left: It has been suggested that the fitting of cameras into modified drop-tanks, to make reconnaissance pods, is a new idea. But obviously it is not, as can be seen from this 30 gallon slipper tank modified to carry an F24 camera and about to be fitted to a Spitfire FRXIV of the 2nd Tactical Air Force late in the war.

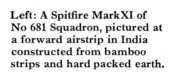

Left: A Spitfire MarkXI of No 681 Squadron, pictured at a forward airstrip in India constructed from bamboo strips and hard packed earth.

Right: A Spitfire XIs also served in the USAAF, as for example this one belonging to the 7th Photographic Group which was part of the Eighth Air Force; accompanying her in this picture is an F-5 Lightning of the same unit.

Below: Tiger in wolf's clothing: a captured Spitfire XI, bearing Luftwaffe markings. This aircraft was operated by the Sonderstaffel Wanderzirkus, a unit formed to demonstrate captured Allied aircraft to German fighter schools and operational units.

Top left: A beautiful Charles Brown study of a photographic reconnaissance SpitfireXI, taken during her flight trials with Jeffrey Quill at the controls. This aircraft later served on No 16 Squadron.

Bottom left: The diminutive Messerschmitt 163 rocket-propelled fighter, which menaced Allied reconnaissance aircraft during the final year of the war.

ground; however, I had no interference over Bohlen and Molbis, the first two targets.

It was during the first run over Rositz that, in looking behind towards Leipzig, I saw two large trails at approximately 20 and 10,000 feet respectively coming from Leipzig/Mochau airfield. Their speed was phenomenal, rate of climb about 10,000 feet per minute at an angle of about 60°. It was not long before two tiny Me 163 rocket-propelled aircraft came visible.

The first enemy aircraft drew up to my altitude and about a mile distant, passing on up to about 40,000 feet before turning off his rocket and becoming very difficult to see. This happened in what seemed to be a second, meanwhile the other Me 163 was already drawing very close and it was obvious that I would stand no chance of seeing both aircraft when they were gliding above endeavouring to position themselves. On the other hand, with the contrail flowing behind me, I was a very conspicuous target.

My first impulse was to get out of the contrail zone; I rolled over on my back, opened up to full boost and revs and

dived to about 18,000 feet where my airspeed was in the region of 500mph, then I levelled out and swinging on a violent 90° turn to port I looked back up my descending trail. One Me 163 was already diving parallel to my trail and when I saw him he was only 5 or 6,000 feet above and rapidly closing. I swung round in a sharp 180° turn as he made his pass, thereby causing us to be heading in opposite directions and drawing apart so rapidly that he was soon only a tiny speck. I again altered course and descended rapidly. The enemy came back to the area but was well above me. Realizing I was not seen I descended to 6,000 feet in a southerly direction; I tried to see the second Me 163, but was unable to do so.

The engagement lasted only five minutes and as I had obviously lost the enemy I decided to fly east. I climbed to just below trail height in order to photograph Chemnitz which was now about 50 miles to the north west. No further sign of the enemy was seen and I had no difficulty in completing my photography. At 1345 hours I landed at Bradwell Bay with 10 minutes fuel left.

The inability of the enemy to position himself owing to his high speed and lack of manoeuverability was, I thought, the most outstanding feature of this short engagement.

Left: The final mark of the Spitfire built for the photographic reconnaissance role was the Mark XIX, which was essentially an adaptation of the Griffon-engined Mark XIV fighter. This Spitfire XIX carried the identification letters of the Photographic Reconnaissance Development Unit.

Below: Now that is low flying . . . A dramatic low-level reconnaissance photograph of a German Jadgschloss radar station in Denmark, taken from a Spitfire. Radar stations were amongst the most demanding of the photographic reconnaissance targets, because close-ups were essential if the technical details of the equipment were to be gleaned.

Above, right: Spitfire IXs of
No 225 (Army Co-operation)
Squadron, operating over
Italy. Flying over the
Appenines, early in 1945.
Releasing a supply
container.

Below:
Bomber Command Spitfire:
RAF Bomber Command
operated a few of these
aircraft, for fighter
affiliation, target towing and
miscellaneous duties; this
example, a clip-winged
Mark V of No 1688 Flight,
was photographed at
Feltwell in March 1945.

Above: This Spitfire IX,
photographed at Luqa, Malta,
in early 1945, carries the
blue and yellow fuselage
marking of No 73 Squadron.

Right: Having obviously
seen better days, this Mark
V was photographed shortly
after hand-over to the
French Air Force. The rear
fuselage bore the scars of
extensive re-skinning.

Right: During the course of her development life there was a five-fold increase in the fire-power of the Spitfire, as her armament progressed from the initial eight rifle-calibre machine guns to the ultimate four rapid-firing cannon. The diagrams below show the approximate weight of bullets and/or shells which could be loosed-off during a three-second burst (in action it was rare for a pilot to be able to hold his aim for longer); the figures are approximate because the rate of fire of weapons of the same type could vary by as much as ten per cent. Each 'shell' in the diagram represents four pounds fired.

(1) Mark I (1937): eight .303″ machine guns; three-second burst, 8 pounds.
(2) Mark VB (1941): two 20mm cannon and four .303″ machine guns; three-second burst, 20 pounds.
(3) Mark XVIII (1945): two 20mm cannon and two .5″ machine guns; three-second burst, 26 pounds.
(4) Mark 24 (1946): four 20mm cannon; three-second burst, 40 pounds.

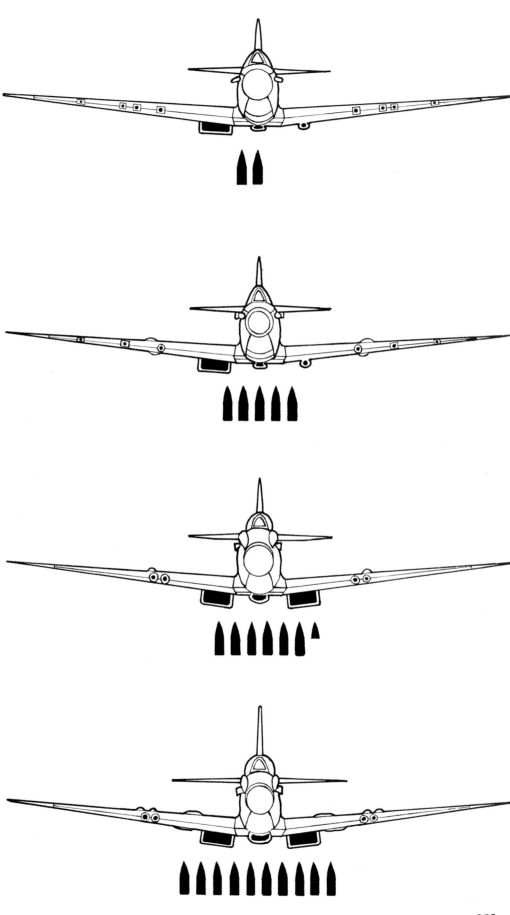

Spitfires over Japan: included in the Air Component of the British Commonwealth Occupation Force sent to Japan after the war were two Spitfire squadrons, Nos 11 and 17. Both flew the FR MarkXIV and operated from the ex-Japanese Army airfield at Miho.

Right: aircraft of the Miho Wing in a fly-past over their base.
206
Centre right: a line-up of Spitfires at Miho.

Far Bottom right: ground crewmen refuelling one of the Spitfires prior to a reconnaissance sortie, during the cold Japanese winter of 1947.

Far top right: this MarkXIV undershot the runway at Miho and ended up straddling a storm drain; men of No 3 Repair and Salvage Unit are seen preparing to lift aircraft the clear.

Below: Flight Lieutenant Ian Barrag-Smith, a Flight Commander on No 17 Squadron, seen boarding his Spitfire.

Below right: Japanese labourers at Miho pushing one of the Spitfires into a hangar.

When Spit
Fought Spit
Wing Commander
Gregory Middlbrook, MBE

A burning Spitfire of No 32 Squadron, following the surprise Egyptian attack on Ramat David.

Above: Wing Commander
Gregory Middlebrook.

Far right: While ammunition
exploded, ground crewmen
struggled to push clear the
other Spitfires in the No 32
Squadron park at Ramat
David.

It was all a ghastly mistake resulting from navigational errors, and afterwards there were apologies. But the small battle fought over Ramat David deserves a place in this history because it was probably the first occasion when, quite deliberately, Spitfire fought Spitfire.

In the spring of 1948 I was a Flying Officer with No 32 Squadron, which operated Spitfire XVIIIs from Ramat David in what was then Palestine. On May 15th the state of Israel came into being and as part of the general withdrawal of British forces from that aread we were to depart for Cyprus the following week.

For a long time the situation in Palestine had been deteriorating, with a lot of killing on both sides. The Arabs and the Israelis were making obvious preparations for an all-out war, to begin as soon as the British troops were out of the way. For their part the Israelis were particularly keen to get hold of modern aircraft, especially Spitfires; they let it be known that they were prepared to pay £25,000 or its equivalent in other currencies, into a bank anywhere in the world, to the account of any pilot who would simulate an engine failure and belly-land on the beach at Tel Aviv or elsewhere in their territory. But in spite of this tempting offer, I never did hear of any RAF aircraft disappearing in suspicious circumstances.

During the final week we completed our preparations for the move, sending out our heavier kit and cleaning out the bar stocks; we sold off the drinks at 1 Akker (about 1p) a shot, which gave rise to some pretty wild parties! On May 21st, the day before we were due to leave, three Dakotas arrived to take away the remainder of our kit and the ground crews the following morning. During the final evening we amused ourselves burning down the Mess and several of the other buildings; Ramat David was in the area to be taken over by the Israelis and because they had been giving us a hard time we resolved to leave them as little as possible.

At this time our main worry was sabotage. For some reason the Israelis thought we were about to turn the airfield over to the Arabs, while in their turn the local Arabs were convinced that we planned to present the Israelis with our aircraft together with the airfield; as a result, we seemed to have both sides against us. To meet the threat we had British troops in a defensive perimeter round us; each night our Spitfires, and those of No 208 Squadron which shared the airfield with us, were drawn up close together on the hard standing so that they could be more easily guarded.

On the morning of what should have been our final day, May 22nd, I was up early. I was just pulling on my shorts when there were a couple of loud bangs, followed by the roar of low-flying aircraft. I dashed outside, but the aircraft — whatever they were — had already disappeared. Apparently there had been two of them, and each had dropped two bombs which had exploded near to the line of aircraft belonging to No 32 Squadron. I grabbed a parachute and dashed across to one of the Spitfires and tried to start her up. But unknown to me, to prevent any possibility of one of our aircraft being stolen, the ground crew had removed the cartridges from the Koffman starter. After five attempts to get a non-existent cartridge to fire, I gave up.

As a result of the attack two of No 32 Squadron's Spitfires and one of the Dakotas were set on fire. Our Spitfires had all been combat loaded with full magazines of 20mm and .5 inch ammunition and when the rounds in the burning aircraft began to cook off there were some unpleasant explosions with flying debris and the odd bullet; as a result, all but one of the Spitfires in that dispersal area suffered at least minor damage before being pushed clear.

Still we did not know the identity of the attackers. But there seemed every likelihood that they would return, so the station commander had the squadrons mount a continuous standing patrol of four aircraft over the airfield. For the rest of the day there was considerable activity as relieving Spitfires took off and those airborne came in to refuel. Because many of the aircraft now needed minor repairs, our departure for Cyprus was delayed by twenty-four hours.

Then, later that morning, I remember glancing up and counting five Spitfires swinging round as though they were about to enter the circuit. I blinked, counted again and still there were five. And that meant more trouble because I knew that at that time we had only four airborne. I ran towards some airmen nearby who were busy working by a damaged aircraft and were oblivious to the threat and shouted at them to get down. Then I glanced up to see a Spitfire diving almost straight towards me — and a couple of 250 pounders just beginning to fall clear. I hurled myself down on the hard standing and the blast of the explosions went right over me; but the rough concrete took a lot of skin off my legs and I still have the scars to remind me.

The airmen I had tried to warn were less fortunate, and we lost five killed and others injured in this new attack.

Almost immediately afterwards the other Spitfires made their bombing runs. It was all straight out of the textbook, just as though they were on a bombing range: they crossed the airfield at about 4,500 feet, each did a 120 degree wing-over into a nice 45 degree dive, released the bombs and began to climb away. They managed to wreck a second Dakota, but by that time the Spitfires on the ground were all well dispersed and camouflaged, and thus escaped further damage.

It had all happened very quickly and, since we had no radar or other means of obtaining early warning, the attackers had been able to bomb before our Spitfires could interfere. One of the airmen did some accurate shooting with a Bren gun, however, and one of the raiders was seen flying away trailing glycol and losing height. But then the 208 Squadron people, who were mounting the airborne patrol at that time, got in amongst the others and the slaughter really began. We learned afterwards that the attackers were flying Mark IX Spitfires — no match in a fight

for our Mark XVIIIs — and in short order three were shot down. You could not really call it a dogfight: it was as though the raiders thought that they were the only aircraft in the sky, and made no attempt to fight back or even evade. The 208 Squadron pilots simply caught them up from behind and opened up from point blank range at sitting targets.

Soon there was only one aircraft remaining out of the second wave — and still we did not know the identity of our tormentors. So the station commander ordered the pilot in hot pursuit of the remaining raider that before he did anything else he was to establish its nationality. Accordingly the pilot pulled up alongside, saw that the markings were Egyptian, then fell back and shot it down.

On May 23rd we finally did depart for Cyprus, leaving the two sides to fight their war without our interference. The Ramat David incident was probably the first occasion when both sides in an action fought in Spitfires. After we withdrew the Israelis obtained some Spitfires of their own, and there would be other occasions when these aircraft battled with each other.

Below: A Spitfire of No 32 Squadron taxiing out for take-off; the airfield was Dawson Field in Jordan, which hit the headlines in September 1970 when Palistinian guerrillas hi-jacked three airliners and forced the crews to land them there.

Swung high
Above the terraced loveliness
Of clouds:
Poised
In the high arched
Vault of blue emptiness
They ride,
Swift minions
Of the Gods of War
from 'Fighters at Dawn'
by R. P. L. Mogg

Spitfires and Guerillas
Air Vice Marshal John Nicholls, CBE DFC AFC

During the Malayan Emergency two squadrons of Spitfires took part in the initial air operations against the terrorists. However the effectiveness in this role, of an aircraft designed fourteen years earlier as an interceptor, was questionable.

In June 1948, when the State of Emergency was declared in Malaya, I was a twenty-one year old Flying Officer serving with No 28 Fighter Recon- naissance Squadron which operated Spitfire XVIIIs from Sembawang on Singapore Island. With those of the similarly equipped No 60 Squadron, there was a total of sixteen Spitfires in Malaya; these, and a few Beaufighters and Sunderlands, made up the Royal Air Force's entire offensive strength in the area.

Almost from the start we and the other squadrons began sending out strikes against the jungle hide-outs used by the terrorists. In the beginning it was a rather hit and miss affair, with one far more likely to miss than to hit. The maps we carried were almost devoid of detail except along the coast; they would show dominant features such as rivers, but after a short distance inland these would peter out into a dotted line with the helpful caption "It is assumed that the river follows this line"! The reconnaissance Spitfires of No 81 Squadron would take target photogrphs for us, but since their maps were the same as our own they had similar problems of navigation. In the jungle one tree-covered hill can look depres- singly like a thousand others.

I vividly remember the first time I dropped a bomb in anger. On July 2nd 1948 I went off with my squadron commander, Squadron Leader Bob Yule, to a target just across the causeway from Singapore, in South Johore. We took off at first light so that we could get in our dive attacks before the usual mid-morning layer of cumulus cloud

Above: Air Vice Marshal
John Nicholls, currently the
Senior Air Staff Officer at
Headquarters RAF Strike
Command.

Centre: Spitfire XVIIIs of No
60 Squadron, pictured at
Kuala Lumpur during the
Malayan emergency

Right: Leading Aircraftman
Robert Collins reloading the
magazine for the starboard
20mm cannon of a Spitfire
XVIII of No 60 Squadron, at
Kuala Lumpur.

developed. When we reached the target area we cruised round for more than half an hour looking for something resembling our briefed objective, before eventually we did attack. Diving from 12,000 feet we dropped our 500 pounders, two from each aircraft, then we carried out a series of strafing runs with cannon and machine guns. There was nobody firing back; it was really like being on the range — except that the target was far less distinct.

During the months that followed we flew several similar strikes. Most of the targets were in deep jungle, and sometimes half a dozen of us would circle for up to an hour looking for the hut or whatever it was we were supposed to hit. Then the first pilot who reckoned he had found it would bomb, and the rest of us would follow and aim at his bursts; after that he would strafe the area until we had used up our ammunition. At that time our intelligence on the whereabouts of the enemy was poor. Moreover, only rarely could our troops go in to find out what the air strikes had achieved; sometimes a week or so after the attack we might hear a report that the target basha hut had been hit by cannon shells, but by the time the ground forces reached it there was rarely any sign of the actual terrorists.

It was all rather loose inconclusive and the reasons were not difficult to understand. Guerilla fighters make the maximum use of all available cover, they travel light, they move fast and they seldom concentrate; operating in dense jungle, they are extremely difficult to find. Broadly speaking, air attacks against them can be mounted in two distinct ways: precision attacks, or area attacks. Precision attacks, by definition, require the target to be visible or to be marked in some way. Area attacks demand a great weight of attack to saturate the area. And both depend for their success upon up-to-date intelligence on the target.

The ineffectiveness of the Spitfire in these operations illustrates the sort of problem we had, using an interceptor designed thirteen years earlier to bomb such difficult targets. Later, Lincoln heavy bombers equipped with radar took over the task of attacking the jungle hideouts, but even with their much greater bomb loads I am not convinced that they achieved much. Indeed, as Vietnam has shown, one needs a bomber the size of the B-52, laying down paterns of up to eighty-four 500 pounders, before one can make any real impression on the jungle; and even then, as I have said, one needs first-class intelligence if one is really to hit the enemy. The best way to go after men hiding in the jungle is to send trained troops after them; air strikes can drive the enemy out of areas one wishes to occupy and pacify, and into areas where they either find it hard to exist or where they are faced by superior forces. The guerilla can achieve his object only if he can subvert the people he seeks to control; deny him that chance, and he will not succeed. It was when we got round to doing that, that we began to get the upper hand over the terrorists in Malaya.

I left No 28 Squadron in mid-1949,

before the Malayan operations were placed on a proper footing. I had had a lot of fun but had not, I think, done all that much to help defeat the terrorists.

Operating against the guerillas in Malaya, we were really asking too much from the Spitfire. But I have no doubts regarding its value as an air fighter. It had that rare quality which comes from a perfect matching of control responsiveness and 'feel', which made the aircraft part of you once you were airborne. You strapped on, rather than got into, a Spitfire; your hand on the stick produced instant control reaction, and it would obey as accurately and almost as quickly as one's right arm obeys the commands from the brain. I have known a few other aircraft with this particular and highly personal characteristic: the Vampire and the Hunter followed by the F-104A Starfighter which, despite its outstanding performance in terms of speed, retained that same unique quality as a perfect fighter pilot's aeroplane. But for me the Spitfire was the first and so the one best loved.

Accidents at the operational training units were commonplace, as some of the raw pilots learned the hard way that there was more to being a fighter pilot than being able to take-off and land a Spitfire. This picture, taken at 57 OTU at Hawarden, shows what happened when a Spitfire tried to 'run over' a Master.

Stronger, Safer, Swifter
Eric Newton, MBE CEng FRAeS

Aviation in itself is not inherently dangerous but, to an even greater extent than the sea, it is terribly unforgiving of any carelessness, incapacity or neglect.

FLIGHT SAFETY AXIOM

In an aircraft a sparkling performance will count for little in the long run, it it is accompanied by vicious handling characteristics. Even the Spitfire had pitfalls to trap the unwary or the unlucky, though mercifully they were few; moreover, thanks to the painstaking work of the accident investigators, those pitfalls that did exist were revealed and in most cases remedied.

After a five year apprenticeship in mechanical engineering, and a brief spell in the Royal Air Force, I joined the Aeronautical Inspection Directorate of the Air Ministry in 1938. Gradually I became more and more involved with the investigation of aircraft accidents and in 1942 I was appointed an Inspector of Accidents; and I have been involved with this aspect of aviation ever since.

During the early war years the business of accident investigation was largely unexplored ground and we in the Accidents Investigation Branch (which at that time came under the Air Ministry) learned many of its essentials from the Spitfire and her generation of aircraft. Of course, if there was an accident and the cause was fairly clear, obvious pilot error or a simple component defect or something like that, then we were not called in; but if an aircraft suffered a structural failure in the air or inexplicably caught fire on the ground, then the RAF would soon get on to us to try to find out why.

Out of a total of 121 serious or major accidents to Spitfires reported to us between the beginning of 1941 and the end of the war, sixty-eight involved structural failure in the air. Initially the most common reason for such failures, with twenty-three instances in 1941 and 1942, was aileron instability. The symptoms were not at all clear-cut: the aircraft were usually diving at high speed when they simply fell to pieces. Only after one of the pilots had survived

Below: A recent photograph of Eric Newton, who still serves with the Accidents Investigation Branch.

this traumatic experience and parachuted successfully were we able to find out the cause. During his dive he saw *both* of his ailerons suddenly flip up, producing an extremely violent pitch-up which caused the wing to fail and the aircraft to break up. In collaboration with the Royal Aircraft Establishment at Farnborough we did a lot of tests and found that this aileron up-float was made possible by stretch in the control cables; in those days control tensioning was a hit-or-miss business, with no compensation for temperature. On our recommendation the RAF introduced the tensometer, which ensured accurate tensioning of the controls; this, and the almost simultaneous introduction of the new metal ailerons, cured almost all the cases of aileron instability in the Spitfire.

The next most serious cause of structural failure in the Spitfire was pilots overstressing the airframe. She was extremely responsive on the controls and one must remember that in those days there was no accelerometer to tell the pilot how close he was to the limit. So it was not difficult to exceed the aircraft's 10G ultimate stress factor during combat or when pulling out of a high speed dive; during the war we were able to put down forty-six major accidents to this cause, though undoubtedly there were many other occasions when it happened and we did not see the wreckage. Incidentally, if there was a structural failure in the Spitfire it was almost inevitably the wing that went; the fuselage was far less likely to fail first. I once asked a very senior RAF officer why the accelerometer — technically a simple instrument — was not introduced during the war. He replied that he was sure it would have had an adverse effect on the fighting spirit of the pilots. Whether that would have been so, I cannot say. But I do know that when they finally did introduce the accelerometer into service, in the Hunter in 1954, and began educating the pilots on structural limitations and the dangers of over-stressing, accidents to this cause virtually ceased.

By the way, I cannot remember a single case of metal fatigue failure in a Spitfire; but that was probably because in wartime they hardly ever survived long enough to fly the necessary number of hours for this to develop.

After structural failure, the next largest category of accidents proved, on investigation, to have followed loss of control by the pilot (thirty-six cases). Of these, twenty occured in cloud and could be put down to pilot error; one must remember that early in the war, in the rush to turn out more pilots, instrument flying training was not up to the peacetime standards. A further thirteen accidents were shown to have been caused by oxygen starvation; on the early Spitfires it was easy to mishandle the oxygen system and if this happened and the aircraft was flying at high altitude the pilot passed out. As a result of our investigations and recommendations, the oxygen system on the Spitfire was modified to make it easier to operate. The remaining three accidents in the loss-of-control category were initiated by the pilot pulling excessing 'g' and blacking himself out.

Engine failures and fires contributed a further seventeen accidents, and the remainder could be put down under the 'miscellaneous' heading. An example of the latter was the case at Hethel just after the war when, as the pilot was starting up an unarmed Spitfire XVI, it exploded and burst into flames. The singed and shaken pilot managed to clamber out, and stood helplessly by as the machine burnt itself out. Everyone was baffled by the incident, so we were called in to investigate. The first thing we noted was that the leading edge of the wing on the starboard side — there was no fuel tank in that position on the Mark XVI — was peeled right back. This was obviously the seat of the explosion and we were able to trace the smoke pattern, like a line of soot, from there to the engine exhaust stubs. Then the cause became clear: the fuel filler cap was just in front of the cockpit, and as a result of careless refuelling petrol had sloshed down the fuselage and on to the wing, and some of it had become trapped in the leading edge; when the pilot climbed into the cockpit the explosive fuel-air mixture was waiting and when the engine fired — bang! Looking round, we found several other Spitfires with petrol lodged in the wing leading edge and this same accident just waiting to happen.

There were one or two accidents, and

Below: The burnt-out remains of Spitfire XVI serial TE 457 at RAF Hethel in September 1946, following the explosion of fuel vapour trapped in the leading edge of the starboard wing; note the peeling-back of the skin, indicating that this was the seat of the explosion.

some very near misses, caused by the light-weight plastic seats fitted to some batches of Spitfires. The trouble was that they were not strong enough, and if there was a heavy pilot who pulled a bit of 'G' they tended to collapse — on to the elevator control runs which ran underneath. We soon had that type of seat replaced.

As I have mentioned, we investigated a total of 121 Spitfire accidents during the war; and a further nine after it. The causes did not always fit simply into the neat categories mentioned above. For example, a pilot might lose control in a cloud and his aircraft then broke up in the ensuing dive due to aileron instability; in that case the accident would have been listed under two categories.

In the nature of my work I tend to concentrate on an aircraft's failings and ignore it if it is safe; but how safe was the Spitfire? I think the figures speak for themselves: a total of more than twenty-two thousand of these aircraft were built, and we were called in on only 130 occasions — and in not all of these was the Spitfire found to be at fault. If one considers that she was not a simple trainer built for ease of handling, but a thoroughbred fighting machine the equal of any in the world during most of her service career, there can be no doubting that the Spitfire was a remarkably safe little aircraft.

In spite of the success of Eric Newton and others like him, in making the Spitfire a safe aircraft to fly, it remains a sad fact that the great majority of Spitfire crashes were not due to enemy action but to simple accidents which did not warrant deep investigation. All too often a hastily-trained pilot's poor airmanship would place him in a position from which he lacked the skill — or the luck — to extricate himself.

Typical of such accidents, and amusing rather than tragic since the only personal injuries were to the pilots' pride, is this one from the files of the Royal Canadian navy. It illustrates clearly the dangers of pressing on in the face of deteriorating weather con-

ditions; and it shows how imprecise communications can so easily lead to embarrassment. This story is told to you the way it happened; only the names have been omitted, to protect the guilty.

A pair of Seafires was flying along the eastern coast of Canada when the weather began to deteriorate and soon the cloud base was down to 300 feet in places. The estimated time of arrival for their planned refuelling stop at Presque Ile came and went, but they were unable to establish radio contact with the tower there. Nevertheless the intrepid pair continued on, well beyond their ETA (and well beyond the extent of their maps!). At last they came to a town which they were able to identify, from the sign-board at the railway station, as Campbellton, New Brunswick — 110 miles beyond Presque Ile. With fuel running short they flew south along the coast of New Brunswick looking for a landing field and eventually found a group of hangars near Bathurst. A low level reconnaissance revealed a runway covered with packed ice and snow and the only landing aid, a wind sock, wrapped firmly around its mast.

After they had inspected the runway, the Number 2 called "Will you have first go, or will I?". The leader replied that he would "Have first crack at it". The Number 2, however, understood this as "Have a crack at it," The upshot was that both did, at the same time — and from opposite directions! The Number 2 later described what followed: "I flew a normal approach from 400 feet at 80 knots over the end of the runway. I touched down on the very edge and when I felt I had the aircraft under control, I called the leader and said "I think I've made it" — but as I said it, we collided . . . The left wings of both our aircraft were sheared off and we were spun around through 180 ."

The leader's account was similar: " . . . I touched down in the middle of the runway and was rolling to a stop when I heard the Number 2 say 'I think I've got it made'. Then we collided . . ."

Left: From wreckage such as this, the men of the Accidents Investigation Branch had to try to piece together the reasons for the accident—in this case the mid-air break-up of Spitfire Mark II serial X 4421 in March 1941. To the trained eye the upward bending of the top spar boom near the wing root, coupled with the tensile failure of the lower spar boom, was significant: it meant that the the structure had failed due to excessive positive 'G' loading, probably due to a gross application of elevator at high speed. The remaining damage to the wing occurred after this failure, during the course of the break-up or in the subsequent impact with the ground.

Curtain Calls

Left: Three Seafire Mark 47s of No 800 Squadron, the last front-line unit in the Fleet Air Arm to operate the type, showing the landing hooks in the lowered position and the contra-rotating propellers. During the summer of 1950, embarked on HMS Triumph, the Squadron took part in the initial stages of the Korean conflict; the Seafires mounted several rocket strikes, and also flew defensive patrols covering Allied shipping. In the following November Triumph returned to England where the Squadron disbanded and the Seafire passed out of front-line service in the Royal Navy.

Above right: The last front-line RAF fighter unit to operate the Spitfire was No 80 Squadron at Hong Kong, which flew the type until January 1952. In this photograph one of the unit's Mark 24s is seen at Kai Tak, wearing the black and white stripes painted on at the beginning of the Korean War.

Spitfire Mark 22s of Nos 610, 611 and 613 Squadrons of the Royal Auxiliary Air Force, led by Squadron Leader J. B. Wales, pictured in formation during a rehearsal for the Royal Air Force Display held at Farnborough in July 1960. A this time the Spitfire was fast passing out of service in Fighter Command and within a few months the remaining Squadrons would all re-equip with jet fighters.

Below: From the beginning of the Malayan emergency until the spring of 1954, the Spitfire XIXs of No 81 Squadron provided photographic reconnaissance for the anti-guerilla operations in Malaya. The final operational sortie by a Royal Air Force Spitfire was flown by this unit on April 1st 1954, almost twenty years to the day since Reginald Mitchell had begun detailed work on the design of his new fighter. In this photograph a No 81 Squadron Spitfire is seen taxying out for one of the final sorties, past a replacing Meteor PR 10.

Left: Throughout the 1950s the Spitfire continued in use for second-line tasks in several air forces, often as personal aircraft for senior officers. The black-painted Mark IX, sometimes referred to as 'The Black Widow', was used by the Chief of Staff of the Israeli Air Force, Brigadier Ezer Weitzmann; the accompanying aircraft was a Super Mystere.

The Final Act
Air Vice Marshal John Nicholls, CBE DFC AFC

In 1963 one of the few surviving airworthy Spitfires was flown in a battle trial against a Mach 2 Lightning fighter. In this section we learn how this came about, and why.

In 1963 I was the Wing Commander in charge of the Air Fighting Development Squadron (the successor to the earlier Air Fighting Development Unit), which was part of the Central Fighter Establishment at Binbrook. Earlier the CFE had taken on charge a Spitfire XIX originally intended for mounting on the station front gate; instead, she had been maintained in a flyable condition.

This was at the time of the Indonesian confrontation and, since the Indonesian Air Force operated a large number of P-51 Mustang fighters, we were very interested in discovering how best a Lightning might engage such an aircraft. In the RAF we did not have any Mustangs; but at Binbrook we did have our Spitfire with a performance which was, in many respects, similar. Thus it came about that our Spitfire came to be involved in a short battle trial pitted against a fighter which was her successor by three generations.

Of course, from the start we knew that the Lightning could overtake the Spitfire by nearly a thousand miles per hour — there was no need to run a trial to prove that. But we did find that the piston-engined fighter presented a very poor target to infra-red homing missiles, especially from the rear aspect. And, since the Lightning would therefore very likely have to follow up its missile pass with a gun attack, a high overtaking speed would have made accurate firing very difficult. On the other hand, if the Lightning pilot slowed down too much he could end up playing the slower and more manoeuverable fighter's dogfighting game and lose. None of this was new we had learned the same lessons during trials flown between the Lightning and the Hunter. Another problem was that if the Spitfire pilot had sufficient warning of the attack he could spin round to meet it head-on — and thus present the most difficult target of all.

In the end we evolved a type of attack which was the antitheses of all I had learned from my own operational experience of fighter-versus-fighter combat in Korea: instead of trying to get above the enemy and diving on him to attack, we found it best to use the Lightning's very high power-to-weight ratio to make a climbing attack from behind and below. From that angle the field of view from the Spitfire was poor, there was a good chance of achieving surprise and the infra-red source gave the best chance for missile acquisition. If the Lightning pilot did not acquire the target or bring his guns to bear on his first pass he could continue his steep climb — which the Spitfire could not possibly follow — and when out of range he could dive and repeat the process. Using such tactics, we felt that in the end a competent Lightning pilot could almost always get the better of an equally competent Spitfire (or Mustang) pilot.

Almost certainly that trial at Binbrook was the final operational act carried out in earnest in the Spitfire's long career.

Below: A fine shot of two Spitfires of the Battle of Britain Flight of the Royal Air Force, starting up at their base at Coltishall. The date was June 6th 1969, and the aircraft were about to take-off for a flight over Normandy to commemorate the twenty-fifth anniversary of the Allied landings.

Spitfire Swansong

M. Maffre

Now there are but a few of them left. Only a few of those myriad Spitfires which once speckled the British sky from the Orkneys to the Isle of Wight, that droned singly or in sections, squadrons or wings across the Channel, that swept at tree-top level or thirty thousand feet from the Pas de Calais to the southern reaches of the Elbe, that swallowed sand and harried the Afrika Korps from El Alamein to Tunisia, that duelled out of lonely Malta and chased the enemy from Sicily to the Gothic Line, that patrolled the aching sunlight in the Bay of Bengal, that teetered like tipsy seamen on flimsy undercarriages aboard aircraft carriers . . .

A babble of tongues chattered in them. Canucks and Yanks and Britons nattered over their radios; expatriate Frenchmen, Norwegians and Poles whooped into their microphones at the sign of black-crossed fighters. Aussies and South Africans drawled at each other at vast altitudes . . .

Grievous things were done to the Spitfire in the name of progress. Her wings were clipped and her supercharger blades cropped for better low-level work, and the outraged bird was dubbed the 'clipped and cropped Spitty'. They added blades to her propeller so that in the end she actually had two sets, one rotating against the other. Lumbering cannons poked out of wings designed to carry machine guns. They put a hook on her tail and called her a sea bird. Once, be it known, she slung beer kegs on her bomb racks and ferried cheer to the Normandy beach head . . .

Today a vintage group of fighter pilots recall her peculiar whistling call as she arched across the sky. Nostalgia brings back the sound of her Merlin engine muttering in the misty half light of a hundred airfields, as crewmen warmed them up at dawn readiness. Some men who probably feel they live on borrowed time, still wonder how her stout iron heart achieved the mechanically impossible and brought them home alive. Those who did not know her may wonder how mortal man can cherish an undying affection for her gasolene-reeking camouflaged memory. And no one can tell them.

Photo Credits

The illustration in this book came from the following sources:

No 19 Squadron Archive: 167T, 17T, 17B, 26C, 33T, 55B
No 54 Squadron Archive: 90UL, 90UR, 90L, 91TR, 91C, 91B
No 92 Squadron Archive: 26B, 27, 34T, 38, 52L
No 111 Squadron Archive: 134U
Aircraft Production: 67R
Associated Press: 43, 147
K. A. Belcher: 89CL, 89CR
Chaz Bowyer: 134T
A. Brookes: 58BL, 131CL
Charles Brown: 13, 19, 53L, 71L, 130U, 131TL, 131UR, 143, 154C
Bundesarchiv Koblenz: 55C, 60, 110, 112UL, 112L, 112UR
Charles Cain: 12UL, 155BL
Canadian Archives: 113C
Wing Commander Costain: 118L, 118U, 136T, 136C, 136BL, 136BR, 137L, 137U
Air Commodore Cozens: 16B, 26T
Crown Copyright: 12L, 13B, 18TL, 42U, 45L, 46, 54TL, 54CL, 54BL, 56 (Inset), 58TR, 59C, 59B, 63TR, 63C, 63BL, 63BR, 84TL, 94U, 104TL, 104BL, 104CL, 122C, 122LR, 125, 126L, 129LR, 129LL, 129UL, 131LR, 133, 152
Squadron Leader Dymond: 134LL, 144, 142
via Ethell: 130
Evening News: 130
Flight: 10, 4, 48, 67L, 70
Flight Refuelling Ltd: 122UL
via Garbett: 58CL (Elliott), 73(Long), 134LR(Nielson)
Girbig: 35U

Group Captain Gray: 28, 86T
Alex Henshaw: 64, 66, 68, 69
Ted Hooton: 154TL
via Icare: 134B
Imperial War Museum: 14, 33C, 36, 40, 45U, 47, 53R, 54TR, 58B, 62, 71U, 72C, 72T, 75, 95L, 84C, 84B, 85, 86C, 86B, 87, 88L, 98, 114L, 115UL, 115LL, 126(Inset)
via Jones: 78, 88U, 89T, (E.R. McDowell)
Captain Law: 106, 108, 121
Alex Lumsden: 22, 113T, 148
Wing Commander Middlebrook: 138, 140, 141
Ervin Miller: 76, 79
Sir Morien Morgan: 94L
Eric Newton: 150, 151
Air Vice Marshal Nicholls: 146L, 156
James Oughton: 52U, 58TL, 89B, 96, 97U, 97L, 101, 102TL, 102UL, 102LL, 102BL, 102UR, 102LR, 103U, 103L
Group Captain Oxspring: 34C, 39
Colonel Horst von Riesen: 24B
Bruce Rigglesford: 146R
via Sargent: 157, 158
via Hanfried Schliephake: 24T, 29, 61, 72B
via Chris Shores: 85TR(D.W. Weatherill), 129UR
Warrant Officer Tandy: 40(Inset)
J.W.R. Taylor: 54BR
The Times: 34B
Topical Press: 55T
USAF: 74, 77, 80, 84TR, 131CR
Vickers: 11, 12T, 20T, 21B, 67, 95U, 104R, 113L